THE
MODERN
WRITER'S
WORKBOOK

SECOND EDITION

THE MODERN WRITER'S WORKBOOK

Marie-Louise Nickerson

BRONX COMMUNITY COLLEGE

Macmillan Publishing Company
NEW YORK

Maxwell Macmillan Canada
TORONTO

Maxwell Macmillan International
NEW YORK   OXFORD   SINGAPORE   SYDNEY

Editor: Barbara A. Heinssen
Production Supervisor: Katherine Mara Evancie
Production Manager: Paul Smolenski
Text Designer: Natasha Sylvester
Cover photo: Slide Graphics of New England, Inc.

This book was set in Garamond and Slimbach by V & M Graphics, Inc.,
and was printed and bound by Hamilton Printing Company.
The cover was printed by New England Book Components.

Macmillan Publishing Company
866 Third Avenue, New York, New York 10022

Macmillan Publishing Company is part of
the Maxwell Communication Group of Companies.

Maxwell Macmillan Canada, Inc.
1200 Eglinton Avenue East
Suite 200
Don Mills, Ontario M3C 3N1

ISBN: 0-02-387480-5

Printing: 2   3   4   5   6   7   Year: 3   4   5   6   7   8   9

PREFACE

The Modern Writer's Workbook, second edition, follows the general format and contents of the third edition of *The Modern Writer's Handbook* by Frank O'Hare and Edward Kline. The six major parts of this workbook parallel the first six parts of the handbook: "The Process of Writing," "Grammar," "Sentence Form," "Style and Diction," "Punctuation and Mechanics," and "Spelling." All workbook exercises are cross-referenced to the appropriate sections in the handbook (see front endpaper).

How to Use This Workbook

The sections of the workbook can be used either in conjunction with the handbook or independently. Instructors may assign the appropriate workbook exercises as students read the handbook. Also, sections of the workbook can be used independently because each area of grammar, sentence form, punctuation, and spelling is explained and illustrated before it is tested. Although it is possible and perhaps advantageous to use the handbook's full explanations and the workbook's many exercises simultaneously, it is not obligatory.

 The Modern Writer's Workbook stresses and extensively tests those areas that should become part of a writer's skills. Its many identification, multiple-choice, editing, and generative exercises enable students to work toward the mastery of punctuation, avoidance of grammatical errors, and effective judgment on word choice. Where possible, exercises include paragraphs as well as single sentences because students are almost always asked to write paragraphs rather than single-sentence responses. Also, cumulative exercises testing several skills appear in many sections and enable students to practice concepts previously covered. For example, after the run-on exercises in the part on sentence form, there are exercises testing both run-ons and fragments; fragments had been tested in the previous section.

 Part I, "The Process of Writing," concentrates on prewriting and daily reading and writing, the thesis, and paragraph coherence. It also contains a newly expanded section on plagiarism. Part II, "Grammar," and Part III, "Sentence Form," can function as a self-contained grammar handbook and workbook providing extensive practice to reinforce correct writing. Part IV, "Style and Diction," offers exercises that parallel the handbook material. In addition, there are exercises on commonly confused words to supplement the material in the corresponding unit of the handbook. Part V contains text and exercises to teach and reinforce use of punctuation marks and mechanics. Part VI on spelling provides many exercises that test spelling rules. In this part, troublesome words are tested in four sorts of exercises: proofreading to identify both the correct and incorrect spelling of a designated word, correcting misspellings in short items of one or two sentences, writing sentences, and writing paragraphs.

Special Features

Additions to this second edition of the workbook include a revised and enlarged Part I, "The Process of Writing", a section on plagiarism; a section on sexist language; and even more generative exercises. The coverage of English as a second language topics (verbs, tenses, voice) has been expanded with increased explanation, solid models for students to follow, and lists of exceptional or irregular forms. These items are noted with an asterisk (*) in the list of exercises following the Contents. Writing exercises and assignments are included wherever possible. Skills cannot be learned in a vacuum; they are best mastered when immediately applied in writing. Therefore, in addition to the many writing exercises found in Part I, generative exercises are also found in the other sections. For example, verb agreement exercises that ask students to identify or edit are followed by exercises that ask students to write brief paragraphs using specified verb tenses. Similarly, writing topics are suggested in punctuation chapters so that students create their own sentences using the punctuation marks being taught. These generative exercises form a bridge between standard workbook editing and the students' own writing.

In addition to the exercises, this edition of the workbook features perforated pages so that students can tear out pages and hand them in; endpapers that key the workbook exercises to the appropriate handbook sections; tabs at the tops of pages for easy reference; a separate table of contents listing the exercises; a completed example for most exercises; and an index for easy reference. An *Instructor's Answer Key* is available to facilitate checking assignments.

Acknowledgments

I am grateful to the following people who reviewed the manuscript of the text: Cynthia Lynch Frazer, Old Dominion University; C. Jeriel Howard, Northeastern Illinois University; Michael D. Reed, University of Texas, Pan American; Pat Bruington Rudeseal, University of Colorado; Evelyn Ann Mitchell Schunck, Richland College; and Stephen F. Wozniak, Palomar College.

Thanks also to Barbara Heinssen, Sharon Balbos, Katherine Evancie, and Ellie Eisenstat of Macmillan for their help.

Marie-Lousie Nickerson

CONTENTS

PART IV
STYLE AND DICTION

PART V
PUNCTUATION AND MECHANICS

PART VI
SPELLING

EXERCISES

I   THE PROCESS OF WRITING

II GRAMMAR

III   SENTENCE FORM

IV   STYLE AND DICTION

V PUNCTUATION AND MECHANICS

VI   SPELLING

THE MODERN WRITER'S WORKBOOK

PART I

THE PROCESS
OF WRITING

1 Preparation for Writing

Good writing does not happen naturally; it comes as a result of practice. Just as athletes and dancers acquire their skills with much practice over time, writers also must learn and then reinforce writing strategies and skills. There are no shortcuts or magic tricks; learning to write requires practice, reinforcement, persistence, and a commitment of time and energy. In addition to your school activities, several activities *done on a regular basis* will make you a better writer. Every day, do at least one of the following activities: (1) keep a journal, (2) write letters, (3) respond to reading, or (4) record observations.

1a Keeping a Journal

In a journal, you can record not only the events of your day but also your ideas and feelings about those events. Here is an example:

> April 11
> This morning twenty students who are protesting the raise in our tuition took over the main classroom building. They locked the doors and won't let anyone in. Most of my classes meet in that building, and the administration has canceled classes for the day. I don't want the tuition raised—it's hard enough to find the money now. But what if classes are canceled for the rest of the semester? I'll have to pay all over again for the courses I started taking this year.

(See Exercise 1-1.)

1b Writing Letters

Writing a letter to a specific person is good practice. What subjects we mention, what vocabulary we choose, which details we include or omit, depend on our audience—the person receiving the letter. Here is an example:

September 25

Dear Mom,

My Classes are going well. We've had two quizzes in the philosophy course, and so far I have a B+ average. Pretty good, don't you think? It's a hard course called "Symbolic Logic." The text isn't easy to read, and the homework takes a long time because I have to think for hours about each problem. But I like it because the way the professor tells us to think is the way I have always liked to think, but before, my friends would always tell me I was crazy to figure things out that way.

(See Exercise 1-2.)

1c Responding to Reading

People who are good spellers and who have large vocabularies are almost always people who read a great deal. From their reading, they absorb the vocabulary and correct spelling. In addition, they are well informed about a variety of issues.

You may not be aware of how much and how many different things you read in a week. The list may include newspapers, magazines, textbooks, letters, novels, recipes, inserts with medication, assembly instructions for a toy, and so on. It would be interesting to make a list of such reading for a week and then to decide which piece of reading was most important to you. (See Exercise 1-3.)

1d Recording Observations

Keeping a record of the things you observe provides another kind of writing practice. Such a record is not quite a journal, but rather a list of observations and thoughts. This kind of record allows you valuable practice both in observing details and in establishing point of view. For example, you might try looking only at the hands of people on a bus. In your writing, describe the hands, and then speculate about each person. What sort of person is he or she? What kind of work does the person do? Is each person happy to have the kind of hands he or she has? Then look at the whole person. Do the hands and the picture they give you match the rest of the person? (See Exercise 1-4.)

EXERCISE 1-1   Keeping a Journal

For a month, keep a journal and write at least 150 words *every day.* A journal is more than a diary because a journal records not only what happens to you but also how you feel and think. If you have trouble getting started, use any of the suggested opening phrases listed here:

The most important thing I must deal with today is . . .

I am delighted (angry, worried, bored) because . . .

I do not want to think about . . .

In the past year, I . . .

My parents . . .

My children . . .

My coworkers . . .

The best (worst, funniest) experience . . .

I would like to change . . .

If I could start all over . . .

EXERCISE 1-2 | Writing Letters

Writing letters (whether or not the letters are sent) provides excellent writing practice. On a regular basis, write a letter of at least 150 words to a friend or relative. If you wish, use some of the suggestions below.

1. Write a letter to a good friend describing a bad experience. Then write another letter about the same experience, but this time to an older relative.

2. Writing to a person who agrees with you, explain why you made a certain important decision. Then write the letter again, on the same topic, but this time to a person who does not agree with your decision.

3. Write a letter to an adult describing the kind of work you do. Then write to a child describing the same thing.

4. After a day when it seems "nothing has happened," write a factual letter that explains how much has really happened.

5. Write a letter to your past self—that is, the person you were five, ten, or twenty years ago.

EXERCISE 1-3 Responding to Reading

For a week, keep a record on this page of everything you read (except advertisements and notices). At the end of the week, decide which piece of reading you remember best. Write a brief paragraph explaining why it is most memorable.

date _____   date _____

date _____   date _____

date _____   date _____

date _____

_____

_____

_____

_____

_____

_____

_____

_____

_____

_____

EXERCISE 1-4 Recording Observations

On a regular basis, keep a record of the things you observe. This record is not quite a journal, but more of a list of observations and thoughts. Look for details, then change your point of view and decide if the change gives you new ideas. If you wish, use some of the suggestions below.

1. On a bus or subway, look only at the feet of your fellow passengers. What kinds of footwear do you see? What do the shoes suggest about their owners? Judging by the shoes, what kinds of faces do you expect to see when you look up?

2. Observe cars in a shopping center parking lot. What kinds of cars do you see? What do the cars say about the shoppers? the stores in the shopping center? the neighborhood?

3. Observe *one* car in the parking lot. What model is it? What color? Describe its condition, inside and out. What does this car say about its owner?

4. Record everything you see in one aisle of a supermarket. First, look only for colors. Which colors predominate? Then, look for shapes. Next, record the words and letters that are visible. What are the reasons for the use of various colors, shapes, lettering?

5. Walk through a room in your house and record what you see. Then crawl around the same room, as if you were a baby. Record what you see from this new perspective.

2 The Process of Writing

A piece of writing is a product that results from a series of actions called a process. The process of writing is complex, partly because when writers begin the process they are not always sure where they will end up.

If you want to build a bookcase, you have a clear idea of its size and dimensions, and that idea guides the construction step by step. Writing is different: It is unpredictable, not always following a predetermined series of steps. There is no one basic formula for writing. Often, in the middle of writing, you discover that you have altered the topic, shifted the emphasis, or perhaps even completely changed the opinions you had when you began. Unlike the bookcase, which will look the way you predicted, your final piece of writing may have little resemblance to the idea you had at the start.

Most writers go through the stages of prewriting, drafting, revising, and proofreading; do not, however, think of these as preordained steps that lock into each other. Instead, become familiar with the various activities in the writing process and use them as they are suitable for each assignment.

2a Prewriting

No assignment becomes a finished paper or essay without planning. For writing, planning is called prewriting. At the prewriting stage, you concentrate on developing ideas rather than thinking about organization or grammar and mechanics. Various prewriting activities can help you discover what you know, what your opinions are, and what topics interest you.

Freewriting can help if you are at a loss for an idea. Set a time limit and start writing down anything that you think of. Do not let the pen stop moving; if you get stuck, write down that you are stuck and repeat it until a new idea comes to mind. When the time is up, read over your writing and see which ideas seem to be important to you. Here is an example:

> I set myself a limit of ten minutes, and so here I go. Hope I can find something to say. This isn't so easy, but the pen has to keep moving. This morning I didn't want to get up, especially so early, but I made a commitment this semester and it's an obligation. I'm stuck I'm stuck. So many people these days don't want to follow

through on their obligations. I wonder why this is. Maybe it has something to do with our modern, throw-away society. Instant gratification. No one wants to put in the time, the hard work, even the mistakes and the setbacks. Instead, they want to be something, to have things, instantly. Like turning the channel on TV to find something they like better.

(See Exercise 2-1.)

Brainstorming is a directed activity that attempts to develop a list of information. The object is to think up as many ideas related to your topic as possible. You write down every idea related to the topic that comes to mind, using short phrases, without editing. Later, after brainstorming, you can edit, rearrange, delete.

Here is an example. The topic given was "When to Have Children," and following are the ideas that resulted from brainstorming:

have children young or later?
advantages to both
disadvantages to both
more money when older
establish career
more energy when young
dangerous to health later
maturity—important
interfere with college
young—maybe drop out of school

(See Exercise 2-2.)

Clustering is a variation of brainstorming. Write your topic in the middle of the page, and as related ideas come to mind, arrange them around the topic. As other ideas occur to you, the ideas will spread around the page. Then draw lines between ideas that seem to relate to each other.

On the next page is an example of clustering around the topic "Dress Codes for Students."

(See Exercise 2-3.)

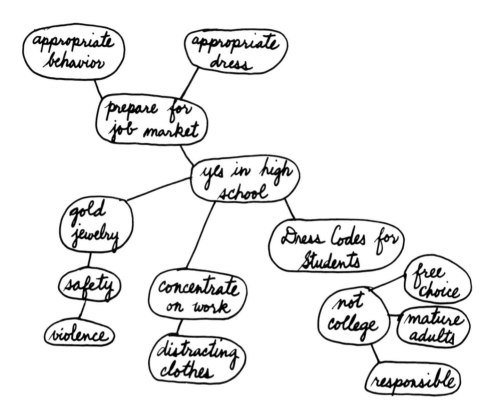

2b Topic and Thesis

Writing a first draft is difficult without a thesis. A **thesis statement** states the point your essay will make. Rather than simply announcing your topic, the thesis statement makes an assertion with which others may agree or disagree. A topic statement tells the reader nothing more than what your subject matter is; on the other hand, your thesis statement tells the reader your opinion, your point of view on the topic.

> TOPIC STATEMENT: This paper will discuss the crisis in medical malpractice insurance.
>
> THESIS STATEMENT: Doctors who are unwilling to police their own profession have brought the malpractice insurance crisis on themselves.

Notice how much more interesting, as well as controversial, the thesis statement is than the topic statement.

If you cannot think of a thesis statement, try *priming writing.* Set a goal of 150–250 words, and write about the topic as if it were the subject of a journal entry. Write down ideas, details, and examples of the topic as they occur to you. In the priming writing, you may discover your attitudes toward the topic, and from those feelings or attitudes you can develop a thesis statement. (See Exercises 2-5 through 2-8.)

EXERCISE 2-1 Freewriting

Set a time limit of ten to fifteen minutes and write down anything that comes into your mind. The only rule in freewriting is that your pen must keep moving. If you get stuck, write the last word again and again until a new idea emerges.

_____

_____

_____

_____

_____

_____

_____

_____

_____

_____

_____

_____

_____

_____

_____

_____

_____

_____

_____

_____

EXERCISE 2-2   Brainstorming

Choose one of the following topics or one of your own. For ten minutes, write down every idea related to the topic that comes to mind. Use single words or short phrases. Do not edit—repeat a word if you think of it again, and do not reject any idea.

TOPICS

supermarkets	a boring job
automobiles	television evangelists
drug addicts	good day care
Thanksgiving	school elections
an emergency room	first-aid training
gym class	college sports
shopping malls	after-school jobs
a famous athlete	large families
AIDS	the perfect job
dorms	required courses

_____

_____

_____

_____

_____

_____

_____

_____

_____

_____

_____

_____

_____

EXERCISE 2-3   Clustering

Choose a topic from Exercise 2-2 or one of your own. Write the topic in the middle of this page. As ideas related to the topic come into your mind, arrange them around the central topic. Then draw lines between related ideas.

EXERCISE 2-4 Identifying Topic and Thesis

Label each sentence as either a topic statement or a thesis statement.

> **Example:** The police department should hire more women. *thesis*

1. The children of famous people lead difficult, unenviable lives. _____

2. All high schools should offer their students confidential counseling on contraception. _____

3. The subject of gun control is debated by millions of people every year. _____

4. This paper discusses the legal responsibilities of establishments selling alcohol. _____

5. English should by law be the official language of the United States. _____

6. Hundreds of crimes are committed every week on the subway. _____

7. Our rigid educational system pressures even its youngest students. _____

8. Almost everyone has strong feelings either for or against abortion. _____

9. Watching too much television adversely affects a child's intellectual and emotional development. _____

10. Although expensive, solar power is preferable to any other form of energy. _____

EXERCISE 2-5   Identifying Topic and Thesis

Label each sentence as either a topic statement or a thesis statement.

> **Example:**   Abortion is an issue that stirs up strong feelings.   *topic*

1. This paper will discuss the effects of alcohol on the fetus at different stages of development. _____

2. Fetal Alcohol Syndrome is a frightening problem that could have severe consequences for our nation. _____

3. The average age of women at their first pregnancy has dropped in the last twenty years. _____

4. Snowmobiles should be prohibited from the state parks. _____

5. All colleges should have a second-language requirement. _____

6. People who do not take proper care of their children should not be allowed to keep them. _____

7. Reading scores are directly related to the amount of television viewing children do. _____

8. Reading scores in the city school system fell slightly last year. _____

9. Reading uses and encourages more thinking skills than watching television does. _____

10. The number of reported cases of burglary did not increase this month. _____

EXERCISE 2-6 Creating a Thesis

Create a thesis statement for each of the following topics.

> **Example:** Schools
>
> *All elementary schools should provide breakfast for needy students.*

1. Nursing homes

_____

_____

2. Computers

_____

_____

3. Day-care centers

_____

_____

4. Mathematics

_____

_____

5. Exercise

_____

_____

EXERCISE 2-7   Creating a Thesis

Create a thesis for each of the following topics.

> ***Example:***   Dress codes
>
> _Dress codes are not necessary in college._

1. Car alarms

_____

_____

2. Dieting

_____

_____

3. Physical Education courses

_____

_____

4. Violence on television

_____

_____

_____

5. Voting

_____

_____

_____

3 Writing Coherent Paragraphs

A paragraph is a group of several sentences, all of which relate to one central unit of thought. There is no one ideal length for a paragraph; one suggestion is that a paragraph should be longer than two sentences but shorter than a page. Very short paragraphs may be low on content and therefore unconvincing, whereas very long paragraphs may confuse a reader with too much information. Rather than worrying about a set number of sentences, you can consider a paragraph long enough when its main idea has enough convincing support.

A paragraph's controlling, or main, idea is usually summarized in a **topic sentence**, which functions in the paragraph as a thesis functions in an essay. The thesis sentence in the introduction states the point of view, the main assertion that the entire essay will present. The topic sentence in each paragraph announces which area of the thesis will be dealt with in the upcoming paragraph. The main idea expressed in the topic sentence is given **support** by the other sentences, which give specific information to back up the controlling statement. When all the details and examples in these sentences relate directly to the controlling idea, the paragraph has **unity**.

3a The Topic Sentence

The **topic sentence** tells the reader what single central idea is discussed in the paragraph. A good topic sentence mentions the subject and specifies which area of the subject will be covered. Look at the following example:

Social skills are as important as intellectual skills in a child's development.

This topic sentence announces the subject, a child's social skills, and specifies the area to be discussed, the importance of social skills in relation to intellectual ones.

Often, though not always, the topic sentence appears at the beginning of a paragraph. (See Exercises 3-1 through 3-3.)

3b Support and Unity

The main idea expressed in the topic sentence is given **support** by the other sentences. Support your main idea with specific, relevant information—facts, statistics, details, examples, illustrations, anecdotes—that backs it up. Every sentence should provide proof. When every detail, example, and fact relate directly to the controlling idea, the paragraph has **unity**. A paragraph lacks unity when some of its sentences digress, presenting information or illustrations that do not provide proof for or support the main idea. (See Exercise 3-4.)

3c Development and Organizational Strategies

Good organization of a paragraph helps a reader to follow your argument or line of thinking. The kind of organization you choose depends on your overall aim. What follows are brief descriptions of various organizational strategies and patterns of development.

Organizational strategies

1. *General to specific*: This form of organization presents a general idea first and then gives specific reasons, illustrations, and facts to support the idea. (See Exercise 3-5.) Here is an example:

   > Bicycles built for two, or tandems, are becoming popular again. While tandems never really disappeared, in the 1990s sales have increased dramatically. In 1991 sales of two-seater bikes doubled compared to the previous year. The old tandems were very heavy and extremely slow; therefore, they did not appeal to serious cyclists. New technology used in mountain bikes makes tandems strong, light, and fast; two people of unequal cycling ability can ride faster on a tandem than either one could alone.

2. *Specific to general*: This organizational pattern provides a number of specific details first and concludes with a general statement that pulls together all the details. (See Exercise 3-6.) Here is an example:

   > In a small city in the Northeast, 62 public school teachers recently lost their jobs. Some of those teachers had 20 or more years of experience. The biggest employer in the area, an electric company, has laid off 3,000 workers in the last two years, with more layoffs expected this year. Another company, a subcontractor making rail cars, let go 56 workers recently. Although economists claim that the recession is over and that an economic recovery has begun, no improvement can be seen in this city. Here, the recession is still in full force.

3. *Climactic order*: This pattern of organization supports the main idea beginning with the least important information and building up to the most important. (See Exercise 3-7.) Here is an example:

The events that occurred in the Soviet Union in 1991 spurred many changes, some small, some great. Statues of Lenin and other Communist notables were toppled and destroyed. The country's second-largest city changed its name from Leningrad back to the original St. Petersburg. Various states have declared their independence from the Soviet Union. In the most extraordinary change, the Communist Party no longer has control of the government and its policies.

4. *Time order.* Organization of information by time order is useful in telling a story or explaining a sequence. (See Exercise 3-8.) Here is an example:

High technology is being used by both sides in the struggle between police and speeding motorists. Conventional radar units are used by most police departments. These units send out radio waves using frequencies known as the X band or K band. Years ago, radar detectors were developed that can intercept the X band. Some police departments then switched to units using the Ka band, which gives a broader range of frequencies. In turn, manufacturers created a detector that can intercept the new equipment. Recently, however, police departments in a number of states have begun using a laser-based system that radar detectors cannot spot because the system uses light pulses instead of radio waves.

5. *Spatial order.* Using spatial order explains the relative physical positions of people or things. Spatial order can proceed from the center out, from outside to the center, from one end to another, and so forth. (See Exercise 3-9.) Here is an example:

Mr. Han's grocery store is both crowded and orderly. Outside on narrow tables are neat piles of newspapers—nationals, metropolitan dailies, and regional weeklies. The windows are filled with advertisements, the special sales announced in both English and Korean. Inside the front door there are ever-filled urns dispensing regular coffee, decaffeinated coffee, and hot water for tea. The first few aisles contain bins of fresh fruits and vegetables. Then there are rows of canned goods and packaged groceries, and the deli and meat counter in the back of the store.

Patterns of development

1. *Description.* Description is a useful pattern of development when you wish to create a picture or impression by way of details. (See Exercise 3-10.) Here is an example:

The town of Grindelwald in Switzerland is a mountain resort that offers many opportunities for both hikers and scenery lovers. The village is situated between two mountain ranges; there are routes and trails for hikers of every skill level. From the village itself one can see mountain peaks, including the formidable Eiger. When hiking, one discovers green meadows, swaths of purple and yellow wildflowers, swift glacial streams, and herds of cows grazing in the meadows, their cowbells ringing.

2. *Definition*: Develop using definition when you wish to clarify a term, to assign a particular meaning to a word, or to discuss a concept. (See Exercise 3-11.) Here is an example:

> Baseball has been played for over one hundred years, but only recently has there been an official definition of the term "no-hitter." A major league committee decreed that a no-hitter is a complete game of nine or more innings in which no hits are allowed. No-hit games shortened by rain or other conditions are considered shutouts, but not official "no-hitters." Until this ruling, shortened games could be termed no-hitters.

3. *Classification*: Use this pattern of development to group information into types or classes in order to find similarities. (See Exercise 3-12.) Here is an example:

> Many languages show a bias toward the word "right" and against the word "left." In English, for example, words and expressions such a "righteous," "adroit," "rectitude," and "right-minded" have positive connotations. Conversely, the English expression "He has two left feet" conveys a negative impression. The author James Lipton has discovered that the French, Italian, Hebrew, Chinese, and Japanese also have words, expressions, and idioms implying that "right" is correct and "left" is wrong.

4. *Comparison and contrast*: Use comparison and contrast in order to show the similarities and/or differences of two or more things. The information can be presented in various ways. You can discuss all of item X and then Y, or you can alternate the information about X and Y. Or, you can do a little of both: Discuss most of X, then most of Y, and finally alternate the most important information about both. (See Exercise 3-13.) Here is an example:

> People who think of ballet dancers when they hear the words "dance troupe" will be at first surprised and then impressed by the dance troupe called Urban Bush Women, founded in 1984. A classical ballet is highly stylized, its steps passed from one generation of dancers to another. In contrast, the work of Urban Bush Women, which incorporates movements from both American and African cultures, often makes use of improvisation. Moreover, unlike professional ballet dancers, virtually all of whom are slender, the women of this troupe are of many shapes and sizes.

5. *Example and illustration*: The pattern of example and illustration is especially useful when you want to make your ideas specific. Each example or illustration presents a real case or situation that proves your main point. (See Exercise 3-14.) Here is an example:

> Too many people have assumed that inner-city children, because of poverty and lack of educational advantages, somehow grow up less intelligent than their more fortunate peers. However, almost all children have the ability to learn, which they demonstrate when given an opportunity. A clear example of such ability is

the chess team from Adam Clayton Powell Junior High School in New York City's Harlem. The school's chess team, named the Raging Rooks, tied for first place in the 1991 National Junior High Chess Championship.

6. *Process analysis:* This development strategy gives an explanation of how something is done or how something works. (See Exercise 3-15.) Here is an example:

> Propagation is one way to increase the number of plants in your garden. The first step in propagating a plant is to take a cutting that is six to eight inches long. Choose a young, green section of the plant, and use sharp scissors. Either put the cut end into water, or treat the end with rooting compound and place in a container of moist vermiculite. Once the cutting has put out roots and some new growth, transfer it to a pot containing compost and vermiculite.

7. *Cause and effect:* Use cause and effect to discuss causes or reasons for certain effects or results. Remember that this pattern of development should fully answer the question "Why?" (See Exercise 3-16.) Here is an example:

> The beautiful hand-carved wooden carousels that were immensely popular in the late 19th and early 20th centuries have almost disappeared; before the 1930s there were 6,000, but now there are fewer than 200. Natural disasters, changing tastes, and economics have led to their decline. Storms, floods, and fires destroyed many carousels; more were torn down in the mid-20th century as tastes changed. Later, carousel horses became collectible antiques; carousels were dismantled and pieces were sold to antique dealers. New carousels use fiberglass or aluminum figures because they are vandal-resistant and cheaper to buy and maintain than the magnificent wooden horses of an earlier age.

8. *Narration:* Narration is used to report in chronological order the stages in a process or a sequence of events in time. (See Exercise 3-17.) Here is an example:

> As landfills fill up and are closed and as garbage disposal grows into an even bigger problem, more communities are becoming interested in composting. One town in Florida has started a demonstration project that takes waste and turns it into something useful. A local crab-processing industry produces yearly two hundred tons of crab shells and guts. These are combined at the compost center with tree scraps—brush, bark, and wood chips. At the end of a year, the result is usable compost, which the town has been selling to landscapers.

3d Transition

Transitional words and phrases help the reader to follow your logic or argument. Following are some common transitional words and phrases and the relationship they indicate.

Addition

Use *also, first (second, third, and so on), furthermore, further, in addition* to indicate which point of your argument you are dealing with or to stress that you are adding another piece of information.

Similarity

Likewise, moreover, similarly are words that signal you will present a statement comparable to one just discussed.

Contrast

Although, however, on the contrary, nevertheless, on the other hand indicate to the reader that the next statement will differ from the previous information.

Time

Before, later, finally, subsequently allow your reader to follow the sequence of events chronologically.

Place or direction

Above, nearby, overhead, underneath give the reader a sense of location.

Purpose

The phrases *for this purpose, to this end* signal that the reason for a certain action will be explained.

Result

As a result, consequently, therefore, hence indicate that a result or consequence will be described.

Example or intensification

The phrases *for example, in fact, in other words, for instance* tell the reader that a statement or opinion will be reinforced with an example or a restatement in different words.

Summary or conclusion

Finally, in conclusion, on the whole, in summary signal that you are concluding, coming to your final point.

(See Exercise 3-18.)

3e Avoiding Plagiarism

When in your writing you use information, ideas, and quotations from outside sources, it is absolutely necessary to acknowledge your sources. It is dishonest to take the words and/or the ideas of another person and to pretend that those words and ideas are your own. Doing so is called **plagiarism**. Plagiarism is theft, stealing; the penalties for it can be extremely high.

One kind of plagiarism involves using the exact words of others without acknowledging the sources—in other words, pretending that they are your own original words. When you use another person's exact words, you must acknowledge the source and insert the quotation (the exact words) into your writing using accepted guidelines. The following example shows first a paragraph containing plagiarism of exact words, and then a paragraph that has correctly acknowledged the source of the quotation.

PLAGIARISM: If the people of a nation are dissatisfied with their government, that government will eventually fall. All governments depend upon the good will of the people. Thus, change will occur once enough people lose confidence in their government's power to protect their rights.

CORRECT: If the people of a nation are dissatisfied with their government, that government will eventually fall. As John Adams wrote in a letter in 1780, "All governments depend upon the good will of the people." Thus, change will occur once enough people lose confidence in their government's power to protect their rights.

Another category of plagiarism involves using another person's ideas (but not the exact words) and again pretending that these are one's own original ideas. Just putting someone else's ideas into your own words does *not* make those ideas your own; the source must still be acknowledged. Paraphrasing is acceptable, as long as your source is acknowledged. The example below shows first the original text, and then a paragraph in which the ideas of the original have been paraphrased and acknowledged.

ORIGINAL TEXT: To the carnivore, the sense of smell is particularly keen and has many functions: it can announce danger or dinner; it can seek a mate or signal territorial boundaries that must be avoided. The faint scent left by passing feet can be detected so easily that a predator can follow an invisible trail quite effortlessly.

Ronald Andrews, "The Carnivores: A Success Story," *The Conservationist*, Vol. 45, Number 5, March–April, 1991.

ACCEPTABLE PARAPHRASE: As Ronald Andrews states, the sense of smell is extremely useful to carnivores. Their excellent sense of smell helps carnivores do many things: avoid danger, find food, locate a mate, or define territorial boundaries. Scents leave a trail that is easily followed, although invisible.

(See Exercise 3-19.)

EXERCISE 3-1   Identifying Topic Sentences

Underline the topic sentence of each paragraph that follows. Cross out any sentence that does not support the controlling idea.

> ***Example:*** <u>The popularity of rodeo, America's oldest native sport, can be measured in increasing prize money, the growing number of professional rodeos, and recruitment of cowboys by western universities.</u> In the last 20 years, prize money at the National Rodeo finals has jumped from $150,000 to $2.6 million. In the last four years, the number of professional rodeos has risen to 800. ~~Rodeo is also the nation's most dangerous sport.~~ Many universities in the West recruit cowboys and offer athletic scholarships in the sport.

1. As in many other sports, the rules of basketball have changed since the sport was invented. In 1937, the center jump shot after every score was eliminated, a change that speeded up the game considerably. Another innovation is the 24-second time limit for the offensive team to attempt a shot. Baseball's most controversial innovation is the designated hitter. Another difference from the original rules is the three-point shot.

2. Comic strips, although primarily intended to be humorous, have also been effective vehicles for political and social messages. *Little Orphan Annie* extolled capitalism and conservatism. *Superman, Tarzan,* and *Flash Gordon* had superheroes as their main characters. Walt Kelly's *Pogo* often ridiculed the enemies of liberalism. *Doonesbury,* by Gary Trudeau, ridicules the follies of modern-day politics.

3. Scientists consider the tropical rain forests of Africa, Asia, and Latin America to be equivalent to an unexplored continent. The rain forests contain millions of unnamed plants and animals, two-thirds of which live aloft in the canopy, never touching the ground. As a result, studying the rain forest is extremely difficult, for only half the trees are strong enough to climb. In addition, poisonous snakes and stinging insects abound. Conservationists are concerned about the encroachment of civilization on the rain forest.

4. Ice dancing is not the same as pairs figure skating, although both are done on skates. Figure skaters must execute multiple spins, air turns, throws, and high lifts, all of which are forbidden to ice dancers. Ice hockey is, of course, a very

different sport. Ice dancing does not rely on feats of athletic skill, but rather creates its effects with a combination of choreography, atmosphere, and drama.

5. Many qualities have contributed to the long-lasting popularity of the peony. Grown in China for 2,500 years and introduced in Europe in 1800, peonies have been a symbol of beauty for centuries. The bushes are not fussy about soils, and they produce lovely blossoms suitable for flower arrangements. Always use a vase proportioned to the cut flowers in any arrangement. Peony plants are long lived; some are known to be more than one hundred years old.

| EXERCISE 3-2 | Writing Topic Sentences |

Write a topic sentence for each of the following topics.

> ***Example:*** Exercise
>
> *Exercise can provide psychological as well as*
> *physical benefits.*

1. Cigarettes

   _____

   _____

2. Libraries

   _____

   _____

3. Vacations

   _____

   _____

4. Retirement at age sixty-five

   _____

   _____

5. Music videos

   _____

   _____

EXERCISE 3-3 Writing Topic Sentences

Write a topic sentence for each of the following topics.

Example: Movies
Movies about historical events are not always
accurate.

1. Fashion in clothing

_____

_____

2. Pets

_____

_____

3. Public transportation

_____

_____

4. Fast food

_____

_____

5. Television commercials

_____

_____

EXERCISE 3-4   Supplying Supporting Details

Give three supporting details for each topic sentence that follows.

1. All college students should take at least one computer course.

_____

_____

_____

2. Being a good parent does not happen naturally; it must be learned.

_____

_____

_____

3. Success should not be measured only by a person's income.

_____

_____

_____

4. Without television and newspaper reporters, corruption in government would increase.

_____

_____

_____

5. One must prepare thoroughly for a job interview.

_____

_____

_____

EXERCISE 3-5 Paragraph Organization— General to Specific

Choose a suggested topic or one of your own and write a paragraph using the general-to-specific pattern of development.

SUGGESTED TOPICS: televised sports, modern heroes

TOPIC SENTENCE: _____

_____

DETAILS

_____

_____

_____

PARAGRAPH

_____

_____

_____

_____

_____

_____

_____

_____

_____

_____

EXERCISE 3-6 Paragraph Organization— Specific to General

Choose a suggested topic or one of your own and write a paragraph using the specific-to-general pattern of development.

SUGGESTED TOPICS: mass transit, college registration

TOPIC SENTENCE: _____

_____

DETAILS

_____

_____

_____

PARAGRAPH

_____

_____

_____

_____

_____

_____

_____

_____

_____

_____

EXERCISE 3-7 Paragraph Organization—
Climactic Order

Choose a suggested topic or one of your own and write a paragraph using climactic order.

SUGGESTED TOPICS: a job interview, day-care centers

TOPIC SENTENCE: _____

_____

DETAILS

_____

_____

_____

PARAGRAPH

_____

_____

_____

_____

_____

_____

_____

_____

_____

EXERCISE 3-8   Paragraph Organization— Time Order

Choose a suggested topic or one of your own and write a paragraph using time order.

SUGGESTED TOPICS: your first day at work, how to change a tire

TOPIC SENTENCE: _____

_____

DETAILS

_____

_____

_____

PARAGRAPH

_____

_____

_____

_____

_____

_____

_____

_____

_____

_____

Name _____

Score _____

EXERCISE 3-9 Paragraph Organization— Spatial Order

Choose a suggested topic or one of your own and write a paragraph using spatial order.

SUGGESTED TOPICS: your neighborhood, a courtroom

TOPIC SENTENCE: _____

_____

DETAILS

_____

_____

_____

PARAGRAPH

_____

_____

_____

_____

_____

_____

_____

_____

_____

_____

_____

EXERCISE 3-10   Paragraph Development —Description

Choose a suggested topic or one of your own and write a paragraph of description.

SUGGESTED TOPICS: the loveliest sight you have seen, your favorite room

TOPIC SENTENCE: _____

_____

DETAILS

_____

_____

_____

PARAGRAPH

_____

_____

_____

_____

_____

_____

_____

_____

_____

_____

Name _____

Score _____

EXERCISE 3-11 Paragraph Development —Definition

Choose a suggested topic or one of your own and write a paragraph of definition.

SUGGESTED TOPICS: friendship, success

TOPIC SENTENCE: _____

_____

DETAILS

_____

_____

_____

PARAGRAPH

_____

_____

_____

_____

_____

_____

_____

_____

_____

_____

EXERCISE 3-12 | Paragraph Development —Classification

Choose a suggested topic or one of your own and write a paragraph of classification.

SUGGESTED TOPICS: doctors, students

TOPIC SENTENCE: _____

_____

DETAILS

_____

_____

_____

PARAGRAPH

_____

_____

_____

_____

_____

_____

_____

_____

_____

_____

Name _____

Score _____

EXERCISE 3-13 | Paragraph Development —Comparison and Contrast

Choose a suggested topic or one of your own and write a paragraph of comparison and contrast.

SUGGESTED TOPICS: two jobs, two teachers

TOPIC SENTENCE: _____

_____

DETAILS

_____

_____

_____

PARAGRAPH

_____

_____

_____

_____

_____

_____

_____

_____

_____

EXERCISE 3-14   Paragraph Development —Example and Illustration

Choose a suggested topic or one of your own and write a paragraph using example and illustration.

SUGGESTED TOPICS: stress, generosity

TOPIC SENTENCE: _____

_____

DETAILS

_____

_____

_____

PARAGRAPH

_____

_____

_____

_____

_____

_____

_____

_____

_____

_____

EXERCISE 3-15 | Paragraph Development —Process

Choose a suggested topic or one of your own and write a paragraph that is an explanation of a process.

SUGGESTED TOPICS: cooking breakfast, planning a vegetable garden

TOPIC SENTENCE: _____

_____

DETAILS

_____

_____

_____

PARAGRAPH

_____

_____

_____

_____

_____

_____

_____

_____

_____

_____

_____

Name _____

Score _____

EXERCISE 3-16 Paragraph Development —Cause and Effect

_____

Choose a suggested topic or one of your own and write a paragraph using the cause-and-effect pattern of development.

SUGGESTED TOPICS: an influential friend, an important experience

TOPIC SENTENCE: _____

_____

DETAILS

_____

_____

_____

PARAGRAPH

_____

_____

_____

_____

_____

_____

_____

_____

_____

Name _____

Score _____

EXERCISE 3-17   Paragraph Development —Narration

Choose a suggested topic or one of your own and write a paragraph using narration.

SUGGESTED TOPICS: preparing a meal, your most difficult task or responsibility at work

TOPIC SENTENCE: _____

_____

DETAILS

_____

_____

_____

PARAGRAPH

_____

_____

_____

_____

_____

_____

_____

_____

_____

_____

EXERCISE 3-18 Transition

Add a word or phrase to each of the following to make the indicated transition.

> **Example:** (*contrast*) She is very slim; *however*   , she is quite
> strong.

1. (*contrast*) Franklin Roosevelt was crippled by polio. _____, he did not let his illness keep him out of politics.

2. (*addition*) The water-main break diverted traffic; _____, many businesses had to close temporarily.

3. (*result*) Three witnesses said Mr. Jones drove his car through a red light. _____, he is being charged with reckless driving.

4. (*place*) Children played at the edge of the ocean. _____, a sailboat cut through the waves.

5. (*example*) He gets lazier every day. Yesterday, _____, he did not even open his mail.

6. (*purpose*) We need a new bookkeeper. _____, we should put an advertisement in the paper.

7. (*similarity*) The subway car was crowded; it was, _____, hot and stuffy.

8. (*time*) The storm knocked down power lines: _____, telephone service was disrupted.

9. (*summary*) Martina Navratilova has won countless tennis tournaments. _____, she must be considered one of the most important athletes of the 20th century.

10. (*result*) The weather has been extremely mild; _____, spring-flowering bulbs are blooming unusually early.

EXERCISE 3-19 Avoiding Plagiarism

Use each of the following quotations in a brief paragraph. You may paraphrase or use the exact words; in either case, properly acknowledge the source.

1. Scenery is fine, but human nature is finer.

John Keats,
letter to Benjamin Bailey,
March 13, 1818

2. A father is proud of those sons who have merit, and puts the rest lower. But a mother, though she is proud too of the former, cherishes the latter.

Confucius, *The Book of Rites*,
XXIX, c. 500 B.C.

3. We are inevitably our brother's keeper because we are our brother's brother. Whatever affects one directly affects all indirectly.

Martin Luther King, Jr.,
"The World House," 1967

4. Women, I have long been told, live within a set of double binds. If a woman makes a charge against a man, the issue will always become not the man's behavior but the woman's character.

from *The New Yorker*,
October 28, 1991

5. A flatterer is a friend who is your inferior, or pretends to be so.

Aristotle, *Nicomachean Ethics*, VIII

6. When any two young people take it into their heads to marry, they are pretty sure by perseverance to carry their point, be they ever so poor, or ever so imprudent, or ever so little likely to be necessary to each other's ultimate comfort.

Jane Austen,
Persuasion

7. Beware of over-great pleasure in being popular or even beloved. As far as an amiable disposition and powers of entertainment make you so, it is happiness, but if there is one grain of plausibility, it is a poison.

Margaret Fuller,
letter to her brother Arthur,
December 20, 1840

8. When we look to the hereditary varieties or races of our domestic animals and plants, and compare them with closely allied species, we generally perceive in each domestic race less uniformity of character than in true species.

Charles Darwin,
The Origin of Species

9. When advertising men still wore gray flannel suits, new accounts were said to be won on the fairways of Greenwich. But the wave of mergers that swept Madison Avenue during the past decade and a half, and the recession that followed, have turned agencies' search for new business from a luxury to an urgent necessity.

Randall Rothenberg, "Seducing These Men:
How Ad Agencies Vied for Subaru's $70 Million,"
The New York Times Magazine, October 20, 1991

10. When you get to that point there is no essential difference between prose and poetry.

Gertrude Stein, from "How Writing Is Written"

4 Combining Sentences: Variety of Sentence Structure

Writing is ineffective when it uses too many short choppy sentences that all begin the same way. Your writing will be more effective and interesting if you *vary sentence structure* by using appositives; adjective and adverb clauses; and prepositional, verbal, and absolute phrases.

Appositives

An **appositive** is a word or group of words that defines or renames the noun that precedes it. You can sometimes combine two sentences by turning one into an appositive.

SEPARATE: The Cathedral of St. John the Divine is the largest Gothic cathedral in the world. It is located near Columbia University.

COMBINED: The Cathedral of St. John the Divine, **the largest Gothic cathedral in the world,** is located near Columbia University.

SEPARATE: Martha Graham was a great dancer and influential choreographer. She wrote an autobiography called *Blood Memory*.

COMBINED: Martha Graham, **a great dancer and influential choreographer**, wrote an autobiography called *Blood Memory*.

Adjective clauses

An **adjective clause** usually begins with a relative pronoun (*who, whom, which,* and *that*). Two sentences can be combined by making one an adjective clause.

SEPARATE: Henry James was an American citizen. He became a British subject during World War I.

COMBINED: Henry James, **who was an American citizen**, became a British subject during World War I.

SEPARATE: Quy works in a Vietnamese bakery. It opens at seven in the morning.

COMBINED: The Vietnamese bakery **in which Quy works** opens at seven in the morning.

Adverb clauses

An **adverb clause** usually begins with a subordinating conjunction, such as *because, if, although.* Two sentences can be combined by making one an adverb clause.

SEPARATE: She cannot take penicillin. She is allergic to it.

COMBINED: She cannot take penicillin **because she is allergic to it.**

SEPARATE: The morning sky was dark and gloomy. It turned out to be a beautiful day.

COMBINED: **Although the morning sky was dark and gloomy,** it turned out to be a beautiful day.

Prepositional phrases

A **prepositional phrase** consists of a preposition, its object, and all the words modifying the object. Two (or more) choppy sentences can be combined by using prepositional phrases.

SEPARATE: Ms. Mitchell interviewed me for a job. The interview was on a Monday morning. It was at her office. Her office is on Lexington Avenue.

COMBINED: **On a Monday morning,** Ms. Mitchell interviewed me for a job **at her office on Lexington Avenue.**

SEPARATE: Mr. Villasenor is an X-ray technician. He works at Hillcrest Hospital. The hospital is located in Pittsfield

COMBINED: Mr. Villasenor is an X-ray technician **at Hillcrest Hospital in Pittsfield.**

Participial phrases

A **participial phrase** consists of a participle and all its modifiers and complements. Choppy sentences can be combined by using participial phrases.

SEPARATE: The governor won reelection. He announced an increase in taxes.

COMBINED: **Having won reelection,** the governor announced an increase in taxes.

SEPARATE: Dr. Eng completed her examination of Barbara. She spoke to the child's parents.

COMBINED: **Having completed her examination of Barbara,** Dr. Eng spoke to the child's parents.

Absolute phrases

An **absolute phrase** is a group of words with a subject and a nonfinite verb (a verb form that cannot function as a sentence verb). Choppy sentences can be combined by using absolute phrases.

SEPARATE: The police exam was over. The candidates handed in their booklets.

COMBINED: **The police exam being over,** the candidates handed in their booklets.

SEPARATE: The roller coaster slowly climbed the steep incline. The passengers screamed with mixed terror and delight.

COMBINED: The roller coaster slowly climbed the steep incline, **the passengers screaming with mixed terror and delight.**

(See Exercises 4-1 through 4-4.)

EXERCISE 4-1   Sentence Combining

Combine the sentences in each item that follows.

> **Example:**   The skater was afraid of falling. He stayed near the side.
>
> *Afraid of falling, the skater stayed near the*
> *side.*

1. The actor is famous in South America. He is not well known in the United States.

   _____

   _____

2. Mrs. Benitez is a lawyer. She works for the Health and Hospitals Corporation.

   _____

   _____

3. She has an aptitude for math. She is also good at biology.

   _____

   _____

4. The immigrants were fleeing oppression. They came to America.

   _____

   _____

5. In Europe cars are very expensive. Many people ride bicycles.

   _____

   _____

6. The broken pipe had been fixed. They could use the sink.

   _____

   _____

7. Jermaine's store is in Masonville. It is a pet supply store. It is located on Walton Street.

   _____

   _____

8. She poured the solution into a tube. The tube had metric measurements on one side.

   _____

   _____

9. He broke his leg in a car accident. He could not play football in his senior year.

   _____

   _____

10. He does not speak Vietnamese. He wrote an excellent study of the Vietnam War.

    _____

    _____

EXERCISE 4-2   Sentence Combining

Combine the sentences in each item that follows.

> **Example:**   The temperature was above freezing. It was snowing.
>
> *The temperature was above freezing, yet it was snowing.*

1. The house was located near the airport. There was constant airplane noise.

    _____

    _____

2. The guard believed the building was empty. He locked and bolted the door.

    _____

    _____

3. Orpheus searches for his dead wife in Hades. Hades is the underworld.

    _____

    _____

4. He reached for a piece of paper. He knocked over a coffee cup.

    _____

    _____

5. He grew up in Switzerland. It is divided into cantons.

    _____

    _____

6. The war had begun. Food and clothing were rationed.

   _____

   _____

7. Many mosaics decorate San Marco. San Marco is a beautiful church in Venice.

   _____

   _____

8. Sam is relatively tall. He is an excellent gymnast.

   _____

   _____

9. Emily Dickinson died. Her death was in 1886. She had published very little of her poetry.

   _____

   _____

10. The children built a snowman. They built it in the backyard. The backyard belongs to the Petersons.

   _____

   _____

EXERCISE 4-3   Sentence Combining

Combine the sentences in each item that follows.

> **Example:**   The television was on. No one was watching it.
>
> *Although the television was on, no one was*
> *watching it.*

1. The copier had no paper. Copies of the documents could not be made.

   _____

   _____

2. She took a flight from Kennedy Airport to Orly Airport. Kennedy is in New York City. Orly is in Paris.

   _____

   _____

3. A pipe fitting was loose. Steam was ruining the plaster wall.

   _____

   _____

4. He drinks coffee or eats chocolate. He gets severe headaches.

   _____

   _____

5. The president proposed an immigration bill. The bill alarmed many people.

   _____

   _____

6. He lives near Central Park. The park is an area bigger than the principality of Monaco.

_____

_____

7. The columnist expresses her opinions in weekly articles. The articles are on the page opposite the editorials.

_____

_____

8. The book was published last year. It has gone through six printings.

_____

_____

9. The dormitory was designed by Ellen Brown. She was a student at this college.

_____

_____

10. Debbie hoped to pass the state nursing exams. She studied diligently.

_____

_____

EXERCISE 4-4 Sentence Combining

Combine the sentences in each item that follows.

> ***Example:*** The fares are raised. Fewer riders use the buses.
>
> *When the fares are raised, fewer riders use the buses.*

1. He had consulted several reference books. They were strewn all over the library table.

   _____

   _____

2. The strike was over. Employees returned to their jobs.

   _____

   _____

3. She built a small house. The house is in the mountains. The mountains are in Colorado.

   _____

   _____

4. Lincoln Center has a complex of buildings. It stands where there were once slums.

   _____

   _____

5. He is afraid of insects. He seldom goes to the country.

_____

_____

6. The high school baseball team won the regional championship. It is eligible for the state competition.

_____

_____

7. The hall had been painted. I had to be careful. I didn't want paint on my clothes.

_____

_____

8. Several students are here. They are students of Professor Quentin. They are in front of his office.

_____

_____

9. Mrs. Grey was irritated. She had not yet received her tax refund.

_____

_____

10. The 1883 explosion on the island of Krakatoa was the largest volcanic eruption in modern times. It blew up most of the island.

_____

_____

PART II

GRAMMAR

5 The Parts of a Sentence

A **sentence** always has at least one clause, made up of a subject and a verb (predicate). In addition to subjects and verbs, sentences may contain the following complements: direct objects, indirect objects, objective complements, predicate nominatives, and predicate adjectives.

5a Subjects

The **subject** is who or what the sentence is about. The **simple subject** is the main noun or noun substitute in the subject. The **complete subject** is the simple subject and all its modifiers. In the following examples, the complete subjects are *italicized,* and the simple subjects are in ***boldface italics.***

> *Six tired **people*** waited for the bus.
> ***She*** read the letter quickly.
> *The quiet **street*** was deserted.
> Do ***newspapers and television*** influence voters?
> ***(You)*** Transfer the data to the other disc.
> ***One*** *of the computer printers* is not working.
> There is *a good **article*** *on financial aid* in the college paper.

(See Exercise 5-1.)

5b Predicates

The **predicate** of a sentence tells what the subject does or is. The **simple predicate** is the verb, which may have more than one word. The **complete predicate** consists of the simple predicate and all the words that modify it and complete its meaning. In the following examples, the complete predicates are *italicized,* and the simple predicates are in ***boldface italics.***

The saxophonist ***played*** *a long solo.*
Her office ***was repainted*** *last year.*
Mr. Song ***typed*** *his report and then* ***handed*** *it in.*
All these buildings ***are*** *part of the historic district.*

(See Exercise 5-2.)

5c Complements

A **complement** completes the meaning of a verb. There are five major types of complements: direct objects, indirect objects, objective complements, predicate nominatives, and predicate adjectives.

Direct objects

A **direct object** is the person or thing that directly receives the action of a verb.

The girl accidentally broke **a window** with a baseball.
The tenor sang **an encore** at the end of his concert.

Indirect objects

The action of a verb is done *to* or *for* the **indirect object.** A sentence that has an indirect object must also have a direct object. Usually, sentences containing indirect objects can be rewritten by putting *to* or *for* before the direct object.

His grandfather gave **him** a watch.
His grandfather gave a watch **to him.**

You told **him** a lie.
You told a lie **to him.**

Objective complements

An **objective complement** is a noun or an adjective that shows how the verb has changed its object.

Ice made the sidewalks **slippery.**
The governor declared the county **a disaster area.**

Predicate nominatives

A **predicate nominative** is a noun or noun substitute that follows a linking verb (such as *to be, to seem, to appear, to become*) and that renames the subject.

Raul Julia is an **actor.**
The game's most valuable **player** was **he.**
J. Edgar Hoover became **director** of the FBI in 1924.

Predicate adjectives

A **predicate adjective** is an adjective that follows a linking verb and describes the subject.

Her attitude was always **positive.**
At the end of a long day he felt **exhausted.**

(See Exercises 5-3 through 5-5.)

EXERCISE 5-1   Subjects

Underline the complete subject in each sentence that follows. Then circle the simple subject.

> ***Example:***   The (customers) on this line want their money refunded.

1. In the Middle Ages most people could not read.

2. Many advertisements in magazines and newspapers contain sentence fragments.

3. One of these children needs new eyeglasses.

4. Out of the huge crowd of people stepped a small child.

5. Amy Tan is a Chinese-American writer.

6. Two of the tires on his car are underinflated.

7. The music at graduation was excellent.

8. Riders on the city buses must have exact change.

9. Several guards patrolled the factory at night.

10. Using a pressure cooker will shorten cooking time.

EXERCISE 5-2 Predicates

Underline the complete predicate in each sentence that follows. Then circle the simple predicate.

> **Example:** I (must answer) this letter immediately.

1. The president's news conference was broadcast live on all the networks.

2. Gargoyles looked down from the towers of the great cathedral.

3. All of these papers must be filed.

4. The personnel office is down the hall on the right.

5. A large delivery van drove slowly down the block.

6. The Detroit bus will arrive five minutes late.

7. A portrait of the first president of the college hangs in Taylor Hall.

8. Everyone taking geology must go on a weekend field trip in the spring.

9. Planting a vegetable garden can lower food costs.

10. Ms. Hernandez works in the prenatal clinic of Harris Hospital.

EXERCISE 5-3   Complements

Draw a line between the complete subject and the complete predicate in each of the following sentences. Underline each complement and identify it as a direct object, an indirect object, an objective complement, a predicate nominative, or a predicate adjective.

	indirect object	direct object
Example: He	told us	the answer.

1. Michael was the first person in his family to go to college.

2. Sir Francis Drake began his first expedition in 1572.

3. His role in *The Godfather* brought Al Pacino fame.

4. Mayor Brown declared the clean-up campaign a success.

5. The director's last movie was not successful.

6. Both Nadia Comenici and Mary Lou Retton were famous gymnasts.

7. The class read six novels by Jane Austen.

8. The jury sent the judge several notes.

9. Heavy snow made driving impossible.

10. The emergency room was full of people.

EXERCISE 5-4   Complements

Draw a line between the complete subject and the complete predicate in each of the following sentences. Underline each complement and identify it as a direct object, an indirect object, an objective complement, a predicate nominative, or a predicate adjective.

> | | direct object | objective complement |
> |----------------|---------------|----------------------|
> | ***Example:*** Exercise \| makes | the heart | stronger. |

1. In 1800, by secret agreement, Spain ceded Louisiana to France.

2. Speaking in public makes me nervous.

3. A strange noise in the hall suddenly became louder.

4. Mr. Torres sold his business to his cousin.

5. In 1989 Ms. Segal became director of admissions.

6. Ms. Jackson offered Tom a job for the summer.

7. The right music often makes a movie scene scary.

8. New students sometimes feel apprehensive and worried.

9. Jazz and rap are two forms of original American music.

10. Maxine Hong Kingston's stories give readers a picture of her parents' lives.

EXERCISE 5-5   Complements

Draw a line between the complete subject and the complete predicate in each of the following sentences. Underline each complement and identify it as a direct object, an indirect object, an objective complement, a predicate nominative, or a predicate adjective.

> **Example:** This handwriting | is <u>illegible</u>.
>   predicate adjective

1. Old-fashioned zoos were basically cages.

2. These cages did not give animals much room or a natural setting.

3. Animals did not have much space for exercise.

4. The poor conditions usually made the animals lethargic and listless.

5. Also, many animals could not produce offspring.

6. Many critics have called such zoos monstrous.

7. In new zoos, moats, rather than bars, surround many animals.

8. Spacious surroundings give the animals a chance to exercise.

9. Natural settings encourage normal animal behavior and reproduction.

10. These new zoos are a vast improvement over the old ones.

6 The Parts of Speech

The eight parts of speech are *nouns, verbs, pronouns, adjectives, adverbs, prepositions, conjunctions,* and *interjections.* A word's function in a sentence determines the word's part of speech. A word may function as more than one part of speech.

6a Nouns

A **noun** is the name of a person, place, thing, event, or idea.

Proper nouns, which are capitalized, name particular people, places, or things.

    Alice Walker   Buddhism   Japan

Common nouns, which are not capitalized, name people, places, and things, in general.

    high school   physics   nurse's aide

Concrete nouns name things that can be seen, touched, heard, smelled, or tasted.

    computer   pumpkin pie   ice

Abstract nouns name ideas and qualities that cannot be seen or touched.

    truth   honor   persistence

Compound nouns consist of more than one word

    orange juice   classroom   sister-in-law

Nouns are characterized by several features—*number, gender,* and *case.*

Number

Most nouns are characterized by number—they can be either singular or plural.

woman	idea	country
women	ideas	countries

Gender

Nouns have **gender**—they are masculine, feminine, or neuter.

boy	girl	child
men	women	children

Case

Nouns can be in the **subjective, objective,** or **possessive case.**   Noun forms change only in the possessive case.

SUBJECTIVE: **Richard** works here.
OBJECTIVE: Have you met **Richard?**
POSSESSIVE: **Richard's** children speak Portuguese.

(See Exercise 6-1.)

6b Verbs

A **verb** is a word that expresses action or a state of being.

Edna **speaks** Japanese. (*action*)
The children **are** quiet. (*state of being*)

Action verbs

An **action verb** that has an object is transitive. When the subject does the action to the object, the verb is in the active voice.

The editor **accepted** your short story.
The magazine **published** several interesting articles.

A transitive verb is in the passive voice when the subject receives the action.

Your short story **was accepted** by the editor.
Several interesting articles **were published** in the magazine.

An action verb with no object is intransitive.

The dog **slept** near the fireplace.
As I **spoke,** he **smiled.**

State-of-being verbs

State-of-being verbs may be linking or nonlinking. They never have objects and are therefore always intransitive.

A **linking verb** connects its subject to a predicate nominative or a predicate adjective.

Business administration **is** a popular major at this college.
Antique quilts **are** quite valuable.

A **nonlinking** verb is followed by an adverb modifier, not by a predicate nominative or predicate adjective.

A deer was **in the cornfield.**
The next flight is **at seven o'clock.**

Auxiliary verbs

The **auxiliary verbs** *have* and *be* are used with participles to form verb phrases. In each following example, the verb phrase is in *italics,* and the auxiliary verb is in ***boldface italics.***

Before sunset, rain ***had*** *started* falling.
You ***will have*** *graduated* from college by next June.
Dr. Stevens ***was*** *taking* notes during the conference.
That Christmas movie ***is*** *broadcast* every December.

Modals

A **modal** is a verb form used with a main verb to ask a question, to express negation, to show future time, to emphasize, or to express such conditions as possibility, certainty, or obligation.

Do, does, did, can, could, may, might, must, will, shall, would, should, and *ought* are modals. In each following example, the verb phrase is in *italics,* and the modal is in ***boldface italics.***

Most babies **can** *walk* at fifteen months old.

I **must** *mail* this package before 2 P.M.

Did the dentist *fill* that cavity?

After a tonsillectomy, a person **should** not *talk*.

Verbs display three characteristics: *tense, voice,* and *mood.*

Tense

Tense is the time expressed by the verb. The six tenses are the *simple present, present perfect, simple past, past perfect, simple future, future perfect.*

	BASIC FORM	PROGRESSIVE FORM
SIMPLE PRESENT:	I work she speaks they write	I am working she is speaking they are writing
PRESENT PERFECT:	she has worked he has spoken you have written	she has been working he has been speaking you have been writing
SIMPLE PAST:	we worked I spoke she wrote	we were working I was speaking she was writing
PAST PERFECT:	you had worked we had spoken he had written	you had been working we had been speaking he had been writing
SIMPLE FUTURE:	they will (shall) work you will (shall) speak he will (shall) write	they will (shall) be working you will (shall) be speaking he will (shall) be writing
FUTURE PERFECT:	he will (shall) have worked you will (shall) have spoken she will (shall) have written	he will (shall) have been working you will (shall) have been speaking she will (shall) have been writing

The modals *do, does,* and *did* are used to create emphatic forms of the present and past tenses.

PRESENT EMPHATIC:	The crops certainly **do need** rain. He **does have** an interesting voice. The movies of Spike Lee **do fascinate** me.
PAST EMPHATIC:	Despite her blindness, Lara **did learn** to ride a bicycle. I **did try** to call you several times. According to our records, Rita **did enroll** at the college this February.

Voice

Voice indicates whether the subject performs or receives the action of a transitive verb. If the subject does the action to an object, the verb is in the **active voice.** If the subject receives the action of the verb, the verb is in the **passive voice.**

ACTIVE VOICE: Ms. Soto **hired** a new computer programmer.
Workers **painted** all the offices in just four days.
We **keep** computer disks in these boxes.
Someone **delivers** the newspaper every morning.
Ms. Jiaou **will mail** an application form to you.

PASSIVE VOICE: A new computer programmer **was hired** by Ms. Soto.
All the offices **were painted** in just four days.
Computer disks **are kept** in these boxes.
The newspaper **is delivered** every morning.
An application form **will be mailed** to you.

Mood

Mood refers to whether a verb expresses a statement, a command, a wish, an assumption, a recommendation, or a condition contrary to fact. In English there are three moods: *indicative, imperative,* and *subjunctive.*
The **indicative mood** makes a statement or asks a question.

The poet Wallace Stevens **was** vice president of an insurance company.
Did Beethoven **compose** only one opera?
Katherine Dunham **is** an influential dance teacher.
Does the Burmese restaurant **open** at noon?

The **imperative mood** expresses a command or a request.

Turn off the lights.
Would you please **answer** the phone.
Keep your hands inside the car.
Would you please **hand** me the phone book.

The **subjunctive mood** indicates a wish, an assumption, a recommendation, or a condition contrary to fact.

He wished he **were** taller. (*wish*)
If this theory **be** true, the authorship of the *Iliad* is in doubt. (*assumption*)
It is suggested that every skier **wear** a hat. (*recommendation*)
If I **were** rich, I would retire and write mysteries. (*condition contrary to fact*)

(See Exercises 6-2 through 6-5.)

6c Pronouns

A **pronoun** is a word that takes the place of one or more nouns. There are seven categories of pronouns: *personal, demonstrative, indefinite, interrogative, relative, intensive,* and *reflexive.*

Personal pronouns

Personal pronouns take the place of a noun that names a person or a thing. Here is a list of all the personal pronouns:

	SINGULAR	PLURAL
FIRST PERSON:	I, me, my, mine	we, us, our, ours
SECOND PERSON:	you, your, yours	you, your, yours
THIRD PERSON:	he, him, his	they, them, their, theirs
	she, her, hers	
	it, its	

EXAMPLE: **He** and **I** will help **you** with **your** work.

Demonstrative pronouns

Demonstrative pronouns point to someone or something. Here is a list of the demonstrative pronouns:

SINGULAR	PLURAL
this	these
that	those

EXAMPLES: The quilts over there are new, but **these** are valuable antiques.
The other store closes at six, but **this** is open until ten.

Indefinite pronouns

Indefinite pronouns carry the idea of "all," "some," "any," or "none." Here is a list of indefinite pronouns:

anybody	everyone	something	each
anyone	everything	nobody	either
anything	somebody	no one	many
everybody	someone	nothing	some

EXAMPLE: **Everybody** should learn to speak a second language.

Interrogative pronouns

Interrogative pronouns are used to ask a question. Here is a list of the interrogative pronouns:

who   what
whom   which
whose

EXAMPLE: **What** were the results of your experiment with fruit flies?

Relative pronouns

Relative pronouns are used to form adjective clauses and noun clauses. Here is a list of relative pronouns:

who   whom   that   whoever   whichever
whose   which   what   whomever   whatever

EXAMPLE: Juneau, **which** is Alaska's capital, is located in the southern part of the state.

Intensive pronouns

Intensive pronouns are used to emphasize their antecedents, the words to which the pronouns refer. They are formed by adding *-self* or *-selves* to a personal pronoun.
Here is a list of intensive pronouns:

myself   himself   itself   yourselves
yourself   herself   ourselves   themselves

EXAMPLE: The actor **herself** had never seen the movies she starred in.

Reflexive pronouns

Reflexive pronouns refer back to the subject of the clause or verbal phrase in which they appear. They have the same form as intensive pronouns.

EXAMPLE: An inexperienced gymnast needs "spotters," or she may hurt **herself.**

(See Exercises 6-6 and 6-7.)

6d Adjectives

An **adjective** modifies, or describes, a noun or a pronoun. Adjectives answer the questions (1) "What kind?" (2) "How many?" and (3) "Which one?"

> **A blazing** fire crackled in **the** fireplace.
> He is **reliable** but not **efficient.**
> **Several** people want to see you.
> **His** essay is about **the** influence of **Thoreau's** philosophy on Gandhi.

Most adjectives have a *comparative* form to compare two things and a *superlative* form to compare three or more.

ADJECTIVE	COMPARATIVE FORM	SUPERLATIVE FORM
happy	happier	happiest
difficult	more difficult	most difficult

6e Adverbs

An **adverb** modifies a verb, an adjective, or another adverb. Many, but not all, adverbs end in *-ly.* An adverb answers one of the following questions: (1) "When?" (2) "Where?" (3) "To what extent?" or (4) "How?"

> The committee will meet **tomorrow.** (*modifies a verb*)
> The Van Gogh exhibition was **extremely** popular. (*modifies an adjective*)
> He speaks **very** rapidly. (*modifies another adverb*)

Most adverbs have comparative and superlative forms.

ADVERB	COMPARATIVE FORM	SUPERLATIVE FORM
deeply	more deeply	most deeply
fast	faster	fastest

(See Exercise 6-8.)

6f Prepositions

Prepositions show the positions and the relationships of various parts of a sentence. Look at the following example:

> Please bring me the book **on** the desk.

In this example, the preposition **on** explains the position of the book relative to the desk. Here is a list of some common prepositions and compound prepositions.

about	despite	past
above	down	save (meaning "except")
across	during	since
after	except	through
against	for	throughout
along	from	till
among	in	to
around	inside	toward(s)
at	into	under
before	like	underneath
behind	near	until
below	of	unto
beneath	off	up
beside	on	upon
between	onto	with
beyond	out	within
but (meaning "except")	over	without
concerning		

A prepositional phrase consists of a preposition, its object, and all the words modifying the object. In the following examples, the prepositions are in ***boldface italics***, and the prepositional phrases are in *italics*.

> Two ***of*** *the plays* we will read this semester were written ***by*** *Eugene O'Neill.*
> The store ***at*** *the northwest corner* ***of*** *Broadway* is vacant.

(See Exercise 6-9.)

6g Conjunctions

Conjunctions join words, phrases, clauses, and sentences. There are three kinds of conjunctions: *coordinating, correlative,* and *subordinating.*

Coordinating conjunctions

A **coordinating conjunction** joins elements that have equal grammatical rank.

and	for	or	yet
but	nor	so	

Shakespeare's children were named Hamnet **and** Judith.
I tried to call him, **but** his phone was busy.

Correlative conjunctions

Correlative conjunctions are coordinating conjunctions used in pairs. These are the most common correlative conjunctions:

both . . . and   not only . . . but also
either . . . or   whether . . . or
neither . . . nor

Both Mr. Green **and** Ms. Gray are nurses.
Whether you pass **or** fail depends on you.

Subordinating conjunctions

Subordinating conjunctions join subordinate clauses to independent clauses. These are some common subordinating conjunctions:

although   since
as   than
as long as   unless
because   until
if   while

In the following examples, the subordinating conjunction is in **boldface italics,** and the subordinate clause is in *italics.*

When *the exam schedule is posted,* students crowd around it.
The hay was especially good **because** *there had been a lot of rain in the spring.*

(See Exercise 6-10.)

6h Interjections

Interjections are words that express emotion.

Ouch!   Oh!   Wow!

Interjections are not often used in writing, except for writing that has direct dialogue.

6i Verbals

A **verbal** is a verb form that functions in a sentence as a noun, an adjective, or an adverb. The three types of verbals are *participles, gerunds*, and *infinitives*.

Participles

The **present participle** and the **past participle** of most verbs can be used as adjectives.

> The auditorium was filled with **laughing** children.
> In the alley was an **abandoned** car.

Gerunds

A **gerund** is a verb form ending in -*ing* and used as a noun.

> **Swimming** causes fewer injuries than **running** does.
> Strenuous **dieting** can harm one's health.

Infinitives

The **present infinitive** (e.g., *to finish*) and the **present perfect infinitive** (e.g., *to have finished*) can be used as a noun, an adjective, or an adverb.

> The lead in the opera *Norma* is a difficult role **to sing.** (*adjective*)
> He had hoped **to have graduated** by now. (*noun*)
> Are you ready **to leave?** (*adverb*)

(See Exercises 6-11 through 6-14.)

EXERCISE 6-1 | Nouns

Circle all the nouns in the following sentences.

> ***Example:*** (Mirella) wants to be a (pediatrician.)

1. Many species of birds are now extinct; the dodo is one example.

2. Alex is allergic to peanut butter and to shellfish.

3. Delicious smells drifted from the bakery and out onto the sidewalk.

4. The researcher's persistence in the face of repeated failures finally produced results.

5. Mr. McIntyre's visit to Colorado lasted three weeks.

6. Some kinds of orange juice have added calcium.

7. Ms. Santana is studying data processing.

8. Several police officers stood outside the courtroom.

9. Tanya's brother-in-law is the manager of a restaurant.

10. Earthquakes have hit California many times.

EXERCISE 6-2   Verbs

Underline each verb and label it as follows: TV = transitive verb; IV = intransitive verb; LV = linking verb; or PV = passive voice verb.

> ```
>                           TV
> Example:    I must read this morning's newspaper.
> ```

1. Snow covered the roads, and no traffic moved.

2. The lights of the bridge were reflected in the river.

3. Alex wrote a memo and sent it to his supervisor.

4. Boston and New York City were the literary capitals of America in the 19th century.

5. The siren of an ambulance wailed in the distance.

6. The election results will be published in tomorrow's newspapers.

7. Alice bought some earrings from a street vendor.

8. The crowd seemed restless during the mayor's speech.

9. At night the college campus is patrolled by security guards.

10. After the movie ended, the audience left.

Name _____

Score _____

EXERCISE 6-3 Verbs

Underline each verb and label it as follows: TV = transitive verb; IV = intransitive verb; LV = linking verb; or PV = passive voice verb.

>   PV
> ***Example:***   This letter <u>must be answered</u> at once.

1. Everyone stood while the national anthem was sung.

2. An early frost threatened the citrus crop.

3. His handwriting is small but legible.

4. The street is being repaved.

5. The shop door opens only when the buzzer sounds.

6. King Arthur is a legendary figure about whom dozens of poems and novels have been written.

7. Most people become irritable if their sleep is interrupted often.

8. A composer composes music; a choreographer composes dances.

9. The small room was furnished with only a bed and a chair.

10. The jury listened intently as the witness testified.

EXERCISE 6-4   Verb Tenses

Underline each verb and name its tense. A sentence may have more than one verb.

> past
> ***Example:***   Despite little rain, the garden <u>grew</u> well.

1. They have lived in Pittsburgh for the last fifteen years.

2. The class will begin at 10 A.M.

3. To everyone's surprise, the project had been completed before the deadline.

4. Ernest Hemingway writes often of bullfights and bullfighters.

5. By the end of November, you will have finished knitting that sweater.

6. He has been revising his novel for the last three months.

7. She was reading a financial report when the phone rang.

8. Delmore Schwartz published his first short story at the age of twenty-four.

9. The elevator was invented in the 19th century.

10. Despite some inconveniences, the New York City subway system does serve its patrons well.

EXERCISE 6-5 Verb Tenses

Underline each verb and name its tense.

> *Example:* By next year, you <u>will have graduated</u>.
> future perfect

1. The pool was closed for renovations.

2. I am trying a new recipe for chicken.

3. Nursery school teachers certainly do need patience and energy.

4. A new computer system will be installed next week.

5. The package will be mailed tomorrow morning.

6. The lab technician has finished the blood tests.

7. A cordless phone can be carried anywhere both indoors and outdoors.

8. Doctors have been testing an experimental vaccine for chicken pox.

9. After snow plows had cleared the streets, we were able to use the car.

10. By the end of spring training, the athletes will have increased their speed and stamina.

Name _____

Score _____

EXERCISE 6-6 | Pronouns

Circle each pronoun and label it as personal, demonstrative, indefinite, interrogative, relative, intensive, or reflexive.

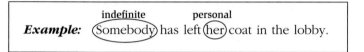

>   indefinite   personal
> **Example:**   (Somebody) has left (her) coat in the lobby.

1. Some of the money was missing.

2. This is my desk, and that is his.

3. The car's guarantee is for ten thousand miles or one year, whichever comes first.

4. Which computer is easiest to use?

5. Nobody noticed that two chapters of the book had been accidentally reversed.

6. Cats usually keep themselves quite clean.

7. Where should we put the glass beakers?

8. The flowers there are annuals, and these are perennials.

9. I myself do not especially care for turnips.

10. Scrabble is a game for people who like words.

EXERCISE 6-7 Pronouns

Circle each pronoun and label it as personal, demonstrative, indefinite, interrogative, relative, intensive, or reflexive.

Example: (Who) left a message on (your) answering machine?
— interrogative / personal

1. Rosa does minor electrical repairs herself.

2. The flowers that I planted last year are doing well.

3. "To be or not to be—that is the question" is a famous quotation from Shakespeare's play *Hamlet.*

4. The children here have had chicken pox, but those have not.

5. Meat that has spoiled should be thrown away.

6. Some people make themselves sick by worrying too much.

7. Do you know anybody who can reupholster furniture?

8. Does everybody have the same ambitions for his or her children?

9. The shy girl astonished herself and everybody else when she shouted out an answer.

10. Who was William Harvey, and what did he discover?

Name _____

Score _____

EXERCISE 6-8   Adjectives and Adverbs

Circle and label the adjectives and adverbs in the following sentences. (Do not forget *a, an, the,* and possessive nouns and pronouns.)

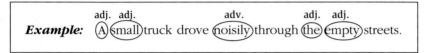

Example: A small truck drove noisily through the empty streets.

1. A large van was inconveniently parked in front of Mr. Jensen's garage.

2. Four children sat on the steps of the building.

3. I think Buster Keaton is much funnier than Charlie Chaplin.

4. Henry types more accurately than Tom does.

5. Friday was the coldest day of the month.

6. An irritating hum from the air conditioner distracted her.

7. Of all the short stories in this anthology, this one is the most entertaining.

8. Several teenagers were effortlessly carrying gigantic radios.

9. Electronic typewriters are faster than manual ones.

10. The town's public swimming pool is thoroughly cleaned every week.

EXERCISE 6-9 Prepositions

Circle the prepositions in the following sentences.

> ***Example:*** Some (of) these essays have been published (in) other magazines.

1. Many of the articles on health that I have read recommend drinking six glasses of water daily.

2. The index at the end of the history book lists all the people and events mentioned.

3. He stood behind the door listening to the baby talk to herself as she lay in her crib.

4. Work on the towers of the great cathedral has begun.

5. It takes twenty pounds of vegetable protein to produce one pound of beef protein.

6. At five o'clock, she leaves work for night school.

7. The messy office had reports on the desk and papers piled on the floor.

8. Secret compartments were found behind the kitchen cabinets and underneath the floor tiles.

9. She transferred money from her savings account into her checking account.

10. Despite his lack of height, he was a great basketball player.

EXERCISE 6-10 Conjunctions

Circle the conjunctions and label them as coordinating, correlative, or subordinating.

> subordinating
> **Example:** He was very shy (when) he was younger.

1. Graduation will be held on either June 11 or June 12.

2. Both swimming and running are good for the cardiovascular system.

3. The operator will not give us his telephone number, for it is unlisted.

4. I don't care whether you type your paper or handwrite it.

5. Although he has won many awards, he is very modest.

6. Do not take the top off a pressure cooker until the pressure has dropped.

7. Spanish, Italian, and French are related languages.

8. Many people speak more easily than they write.

9. She wanted to return some books, but the library was closed.

10. Nero fiddled while Rome burned.

EXERCISE 6-11 | Verbals

Circle each verbal and label it as participle, gerund, or infinitive.

> *Example:* (Exercising) regularly controls one's weight.
>
> gerund

1. Shouting demonstrators stood outside the governor's office.

2. Mozart started composing as a young child.

3. Stretching helps athletes avoid injuries.

4. They hoped to marry, but they were too young.

5. It was not time to start, but she was impatient to leave for vacation.

6. An experienced parent can tell when a child is becoming ill.

7. She plans to rest and to visit relatives this summer.

8. Dust and cobwebs filled the deserted attic.

9. He wanted to have retired by now, but it was not possible.

10. Years of dancing had made her strong and flexible.

EXERCISE 6-12   All Parts of Speech

Identify each italicized word as a noun, verb, pronoun, adjective, adverb, preposition, conjunction, interjection, participle, gerund, or infinitive.

>   pronoun   infinitive   preposition noun
> **Example:**   *He* wanted *to be* grand marshall *of* the *parade*, but the
>
>   verb
>   committee *elected* someone else.

1. The lab *assistant carefully* poured mercury *into* the *narrow* tube.

2. A group of *dancing* bears *performed* in the center ring *of* the *circus*.

3. *He* wanted *to sleep, but* he had *work* to do.

4. *Although* it *seems illogical, exercising* can give a person *energy*.

5. *The* weather was *extremely* cold, *so many* shrubs *were killed*.

6. A *famous* quotation *claims* that *to err* is *human*.

7. *Painting* is *her favorite* hobby.

8. *Great!* Because *of* the *blizzard*, schools *are closed!*

9. *Down* the *block* we *could see* a group of *excited* children.

10. *Her* musical *ability won* her a *scholarship*.

EXERCISE 6-13 All Parts of Speech

Identify each italicized word as a noun, verb, pronoun, adjective, adverb, preposition, conjunction, interjection, participle, gerund, or infinitive.

>   adjective   adverb   noun
> **Example:**   A *worried* man was looking *frantically* through the *files*.

1. People *who* want *to hunt* must get a *license*.

2. *At* Hancock Shaker *Village*, there *is* a *round* barn *that* is *extremely unusual*.

3. Many *of* Van Gogh's *paintings* have *very* thick *layers* of paint.

4. *Ouch!* This *splinter in my* thumb *hurts*.

5. *Either* Bob *or* Ann can drive *you to* the train *station*.

6. *Parents* should *never* leave *small* children *unattended* in shopping *carts*.

7. *Being bilingual* can be *a* great *advantage*.

8. William wanted *to go* to *Virginia* for spring vacation, *but* he could not rear-range *his* work *schedule*.

9. Ms. Green is *actively* campaigning *for* the office *of* state *senator*.

10. The *Berkshires are* a *very popular* vacation spot in *both* summer *and* winter.

EXERCISE 6-14 Writing and Parts of Speech

Write a sentence using each suggested part of speech.

> **Example:** intensity—noun
>
> *The firefighters were driven back by the*
>
> *intensity of the heat.*

1. translates—verb

   _____

2. themselves—pronoun

   _____

3. sturdy—adjective

   _____

4. seldom—adverb

   _____

5. between—preposition

   _____

6. yet—conjunction

   _____

7. broken—participle

   _____

8. writing—gerund (use as a noun)

_____

9. to observe—infinitive

_____

10. fortunately—adverb

_____

7   Phrases

A **phrase** is a group of words without a subject or predicate that functions as a single part of speech.

7a Prepositional Phrases

A **prepositional phrase** consists of a preposition, its object, and all the words modifying the object. In the following examples, the prepositional phrases are in *italics*, and the prepositions and their objects are in ***boldface italics.*** Most prepositional phrases function as an adjective or an adverb.

> The books ***on*** *the lower* ***shelves*** need new bindings. (*adjective*)
> This meat is unfit ***for*** *human* ***consumption.*** (*adverb*)
> The war photographs showed scenes ***of*** *appalling* ***destruction.*** (*adjective*)
> Peanuts do not grow well ***in*** *northern* ***climates.*** (*adverb*)

7b Verbal Phrases

A **verbal phrase** consists of a verbal and all its complements and modifiers. The three types of verbal phrases are *participial phrases, gerund phrases,* and *infinitive phrases.*

Participial phrases

A **participial phrase** consists of a participle and all its modifiers and complements. It acts as an adjective. In the following examples, the participial phrases are in *italics,* and the participles are in ***boldface italics.***

> Mosquitoes ***attracted*** *by the light* clustered at the screen door.
> The stores were crowded with people ***finishing*** *their Christmas shopping.*

Children ***hurrying*** *home from school* ran along the street.
The road crew cleared away a tree ***felled*** *by lightning.*

A participle modifying its own subject creates an absolute phrase, which is always set off from its sentence by a comma.

*His car **having broken** down,* Mr. Harper could not go to Harrisburg for Thanksgiving.

Gerund phrases

A **gerund phrase** consists of a gerund and all its modifiers and complements. It acts as a noun. In the following examples, the gerund phrases are in *italics* and the gerunds are in ***boldface italics.***

Cooking *some types of beans* takes a long time.
She does not recommend ***using*** *chemical sprays in the garden.*
Solving *the complicated math problem* took her only five minutes.
Mr. Agi enjoys ***demonstrating*** *the new computer's capabilities.*

Infinitive phrases

An **infinitive phrase** consists of the present infinitive or the present perfect infinitive and all its modifiers and complements. It acts as a noun, an adjective, or an adverb. In the following examples, the infinitive phrases are in *italics,* and the infinitives are in ***boldface italics.***

To accept *the consequences of one's actions* is a sign of maturity. (*noun*)
Which is the best way ***to get*** *to Phoenix?* (*adjective*)
He was proud ***to have finished*** *high school.* (*adverb*)

(See Exercises 7-1 and 7-2.)

Name _____

Score _____

EXERCISE 7-1   Phrases

Circle each phrase and identify it as a prepositional, participial, gerund, or infinitive phrase.

> **Example:** She has always liked (knitting sweaters.)
> *gerund phrase*

1. Max started playing basketball when he was in elementary school.

2. People marooned by the flood were picked up by rescue workers in boats.

3. He has learned to accept criticism without resentment.

4. I was sorry to have missed your phone call.

5. Wearing a hat will protect you from the sun when you work outdoors.

6. The sun having set, the temperature fell quickly.

7. Proofreading one's own writing is much harder than proofreading another's work.

8. Many people waiting to board the train stood on the platform.

9. Her two goals are to finish law school and to become an assistant district attorney.

10. Gymnasts trained in Rumania have won many gold medals at the Olympics.

EXERCISE 7-2 Writing Using Phrases

Identify each phrase as a prepositional, participial, gerund, or infinitive phrase. Then use the phrase in a sentence.

> **Example:** cutting up the fallen tree ___*gerund*___
>
> *Cutting up the fallen tree took all morning.*

1. to give up an established habit _____

_____

2. parked in the driveway _____

_____

3. at the clinic _____

_____

4. to forgive _____

_____

5. wearing a green collar _____

_____

6. filling out income tax forms _____

_____

7. to have missed your visit _____

_____

8. made of stainless steel _____

_____

9. registering to vote _____

_____

10. beyond the third traffic light _____

_____

8 Clauses

A **clause** is a group of words with a subject and a predicate. A clause may be *independent* or *dependent* (subordinate).

8a Independent Clauses

An **independent clause** has a subject and a predicate and expresses a complete thought. Therefore, it can stand alone as a simple sentence.

> Nathaniel Hawthorne and Herman Melville were friends.
> James Baldwin lived much of his life in France.

8b Dependent Clauses

A **dependent (subordinate) clause** has a subject and a predicate. It does not express a complete thought and therefore must be attached to or be part of an independent clause. A dependent clause usually begins with a subordinating conjunction or a relative pronoun. There are three kinds of dependent clauses: *adjective, adverb,* and *noun clauses.*

Adjective clauses

An **adjective clause,** or **relative clause,** modifies a noun or a pronoun. Usually, an adjective clause begins with a relative pronoun (*who, whose, whom, that, which*) or a relative adverb (*when, where, why*). In the following examples, the adjective clauses are in **boldface,** and the nouns or pronouns modified are in *italics*.

> The water *heater,* **which was installed five years ago,** needs a new thermostat.
> *Those* **who want to take physics** should talk to Professor Miller.

The *intersection* **where the accident occurred** needs a traffic light, not just stop signs.

The young skater finally mastered the triple toe loop, **which made him very proud.**

In the last preceding example, the adjective clause modifies the entire idea expressed in the independent clause that comes before it.

Adverb clauses

An **adverb clause** usually modifies the verb in another clause, although sometimes it modifies an adjective or an adverb. An adverb clause usually begins with a subordinating conjunction showing the relation between the adverb clause and the word it modifies. In the following examples, the adverb clauses are in **boldface,** and the word or words modified are in *italics*.

He *joined* the forestry service **because he wanted to work outdoors.** (*modifies the verb* joined)

She is *taller* **than I am.** (*modifies the adjective* taller)

Martin types *more accurately* **than Nick (does).** (*modifies the comparative adverb* more accurately)

In the last preceding example, the verb *does* may be omitted.

Noun clauses

A **noun clause** acts as a noun, so it functions as a subject, object, or predicate nominative. Usually, a noun clause begins with one of the following subordinating words: *that, how, what, whatever, whenever, wherever, whichever, who, whoever, where, why.* In the examples that follow, the noun clauses are in **boldface.**

That the jury would find him not guilty seemed possible. (*subject*)

The governor explained **why taxes would be raised.** (*direct object*)

The winner will be **whoever guesses the number of jelly beans in the jar.** (*predicate nominative*)

(See Exercises 8-1 through 8-4.)

EXERCISE 8-1   Clauses

Underline each independent clause. Put parentheses around each dependent clause and label it as an adjective, adverb, or noun clause.

> adverb clause
> *Example:*   Registration went faster (after it was computerized.)

1. The small house where Edgar Allan Poe once lived is now a museum.

2. They have no pets because their children are allergic to dog and cat hair.

3. The person who borrowed my calculator should return it.

4. No one knew why the buses were late.

5. That the president would have to resign become obvious.

6. The town grew when an airplane manufacturer built a new factory there.

7. The legend of Persephone describes a time when there was no winter.

8. Give these forms to Ms. Robinson, whose office is down the hall.

9. Students may choose whichever curriculum they like.

10. This car runs more efficiently than any of the others.

EXERCISE 8-2 Clauses

Underline each independent clause. Put parentheses around each dependent clause and label it as an adjective, adverb, or noun clause.

> **Example:** He did not know (that the office was closed.)
> — *noun clause*

1. Ms. Brinkley had to look for a new job after the store went out of business.

2. The college, which was founded before the American Revolution, has become a huge university.

3. His chief worry is how he will pay next year's tuition.

4. Cars pulled to one side so that the ambulance could pass.

5. This professor's sections are more popular than those of other teachers.

6. The reason why Nguyen was promoted is obvious.

7. The plumber, whom she called at 7 A.M., arrived at 3 P.M.

8. A puzzling question is what happened to the lost colony in Virginia.

9. The flash attachment on the camera will not work unless the batteries are fresh.

10. What became of Judge Crater is unknown.

EXERCISE 8-3 Clauses

Underline each independent clause. Put parentheses around each dependent clause and label it as an adjective, adverb, or noun clause.

> adjective clause
> ***Example:*** The Harlem School of the Arts, (which was founded in 1964,) currently has 1,500 students.

1. That the hurricane would do a great deal of damage seemed certain.

2. Athletes who wish to compete in the Olympics must train for years.

3. Fidel Castro of Cuba has ruled longer than any other Western Hemisphere leader has.

4. The computer was even more useful after she had installed another memory board.

5. Scientists claim that smallpox has been virtually eliminated.

6. The factory, which was built thirty years ago, needs extensive renovations.

7. She will receive her degree as soon as she has completed three more credits.

8. The article states that the various Chinese languages have dozens of words for "rice."

9. The police are looking for the people who vandalized the swimming pool in the park.

10. Vegetable prices were high because a drought had caused crop failures.

EXERCISE 8-4 Writing with Clauses

Write complete sentences using the indicated dependent clauses.

> ***Example:*** that the hardware store sold extension cords
>
> *When I called, the owner assured me that the hardware store sold extension cords.*

1. because she speaks both Spanish and Japanese

   _____

2. whoever forgot to lock the computer room

   _____

3. when Liz took a course in Afro-Haitian dance

   _____

4. why the train was delayed for an hour

   _____

5. which happened several months ago

   _____

6. that the candidates for senator should address the issues

   _____

7. although she is eighty years old

   _____

8. who were waiting for the subway

   _____

9. before the air conditioning was turned on

_____

10. where the statue of Franklin used to stand

_____

9 Kinds of Sentences

There are four basic types of sentences: *simple, compound, complex,* and *compound-complex.*

9a Simple Sentences

A **simple sentence** has one independent clause and no dependent clause.

As well as plays, Shakespeare wrote sonnets and other poems.
She is studying the effect of regular exercise on blood pressure.

9b Compound Sentences

A **compound sentence** has two or more independent clauses and no dependent clause.

She wanted to check the progress of her experiment, but the biology lab was closed.
Simultaneously, the alarm clock went off, the telephone rang, and the front doorbell chimed.
Many cities have canals; Venice, however, is the most famous.

9c Complex Sentences

A **complex sentence** has one independent clause and one or more dependent clauses. In the following examples, the independent clauses are in **boldface,** and the dependent clauses are in *italics.*

Because peanuts require a long, warm growing season, **they do not do well in the North.**

The audience applauded wildly *as soon as the baritone finished singing his aria.*

9d Compound-Complex Sentences

A **compound-complex sentence** has two or more independent clauses and one or more dependent clauses. In the following examples, the independent clauses are in **boldface,** and the dependent clauses are in *italics.*

After he spent a year in the Peace Corps, **Warren went to business school,** and **then he decided to become a doctor.**

Students *who want to major in nursing* **must take math and science; courses in written and oral communication are also highly recommended.**

(See Exercises 9-1 through 9-3.)

EXERCISE 9-1 | Sentence Types

Identify each sentence that follows as simple, compound, complex, or compound-complex.

> **Example:** They started skiing after they moved to Vermont. *complex*

1. Because she has diabetes, Mary has to watch her diet carefully._____

2. The Nile River is more than a means of transportation; for centuries, its floods have fertilized the fields of Egypt._____

3. An airport and a school are among many places named for Mayor LaGuardia of New York City._____

4. Many parents feel that children need room to play, so they move from the city to the suburbs._____

5. A large percent of the budget at the office goes for electricity, heating, and the telephone system._____

6. The spring fair will be held next Saturday unless it rains._____

7. Even though he had had polio, Franklin Roosevelt refused to live a limited life; he entered politics in New York State and later became president of the United States._____

8. Jockeys must keep their weight down, or they will lose their jobs._____

9. Maya Angelou, who was a dancer in her youth, is an acclaimed writer.____

10. Despite being both deaf and blind, Helen Keller learned to read not only English but also French._____

EXERCISE 9-2   Sentence Types

Identify each sentence that follows as simple, compound, complex, or compound-complex.

> **Example:** Thirty people stood patiently in line at the grocery store.
>
> *simple*

1. The rustic cabin was not insulated, nor did it have indoor plumbing._____

2. When VCRs became popular, the movie industry felt threatened, but more movies are being made now than in the past twenty years._____

3. Whoever wants this ticket to the baseball game may have it._____

4. The photographs illustrating the lead story in this morning's paper are magnificent._____

5. In some states, people may apply for a driver's license when they are sixteen years old._____

6. Two new stores have opened on this block, and another business will open next month._____

7. One of Edgar Allan Poe's biographers made deliberate misstatements about the writer._____

8. Columbus thought he had landed in India, so he called the inhabitants Indians._____

9. Elizabeth Cady Stanton was interested in the law, but in the 19th century the law profession did not welcome women._____

10. Lincoln Steffens, who began his career as a police reporter, became one of America's greatest journalists._____

EXERCISE 9-3 Writing Using Sentence Types

On separate paper, write the indicated type of sentence using the suggested topics.

> **Example:** Sentence type: compound
> Topic: your parents
>
> *My mother came from Trinidad, and my father was born in England.*

1. Sentence type: simple

   Topic: your favorite kind of cooking

2. Sentence type: compound

   Topic: two kinds of students at your college

3. Sentence type: complex

   Topic: a movie you enjoyed

4. Sentence type: compound-complex

   Topic: a movie you hated

5. Sentence type: simple

   Topic: the weather this morning

6. Sentence type: compound

   Topic: your first actions every morning

7. Sentence type: complex

   Topic: learning a new language

8. Sentence type: compound-complex

   Topic: teaching someone (or learning) how to drive

9. Sentence type: compound

   Topic: your first job

10. Sentence type: complex

    Topic: very crowded buses

PART III

SENTENCE FORM

10 Sentence Fragments

A **sentence fragment** is an unfinished sentence that does not express a complete idea. Most fragments can be corrected by adding the missing material or by connecting the fragment to an independent clause. Following are some examples.

The following fragment needs a subject.

NOT: Drove the car to the gas station.
BUT: **She** drove the car to the gas station.

The next fragment needs a predicate, a verb.

NOT: Tenants from every building at the block party.
BUT: Tenants from every building **were** at the block party.

The following fragment needs an auxiliary verb.

NOT: People leaning out their windows.
BUT: People **were** leaning out their windows.

The next fragment is a phrase that should be connected to an independent clause.

NOT: Keeping carefully to the side.
BUT: Keeping carefully to the side, **Bobby rode his bicycle down the road.**

The next fragment is a dependent clause. It can be corrected by (1) removing the subordinating word, or (2) connecting it to an independent clause.

NOT: Because she knows several computer-programming languages.
BUT: She knows several computer-programming languages.
OR: **She had no trouble finding a job** because she knows several computer-programming languages.

(See Exercises 10-1 through 10-5.)

EXERCISE 10-1   Fragments

On separate paper, revise the following items to eliminate sentence fragments. Two items have no fragments.

> **_Example:_**   Because the bus broke down. He was late to work.
>
> _Because the bus broke down, he was late to work._

1. Several people sitting in the waiting room.

2. Worked downtown for six years.

3. As the temperature fell, the rain turned to snow.

4. The runners in warm-up suits.

5. Because they love basketball. They always buy season tickets for the Celtics.

6. Keeping carefully to the side of the road.

7. Since he learned several computer languages.

8. These work boots have reinforced toes.

9. Hoping to keep warm. He wore two sweaters.

10. Quincy Jones, a person of great talent and achievement.

EXERCISE 10-2	Fragments

On separate paper, revise the following items to eliminate sentence fragments. One item has no fragments.

> ***Example:*** This neighborhood a good place to live.
>
> *This neighborhood is a good place to live.*

1. Michael Jordan an extraordinary athlete.

2. Because mice had chewed the electric wires.

3. For our accounting class. We need a special notebook.

4. The two hundredth anniversary of the American Constitution in 1987.

5. The baby smiled happily.

6. Carefully watched every person walking by.

7. A magazine article describing good health habits.

8. Smart parents childproof their homes. Long before their babies start crawling.

9. Compared to professional baseball and basketball players. Professional football players do not earn huge salaries.

10. Italian and French have many similar phrases. Because these two languages developed from the same source, Latin.

EXERCISE 10-3 Fragments

On separate paper, revise the following items to eliminate sentence fragments. One item has no fragments.

> ***Example:***   Also encouraged her to apply to college.
>
> *Her friends also encouraged her to apply to college.*

1. Wood stoves should not be too near a wall. Because the wall will overheat and catch fire.

2. Ms. Ramos works full time. In addition to attending college at night.

3. Hoped to be working at a radio station when she graduated.

4. Most of the phone calls this morning wrong numbers.

5. Driving along the street. I saw some boys playing stickball.

6. Several pages of the report to be retyped.

7. Even though Frank is quite thin, he is strong.

8. After the Allies broke the Enigma Code during World War II. They had important information about German troop movements.

9. Edgar Allan Poe was an American writer. Who wrote short stories, poetry, and literary criticism.

10. After doing the laundry. Frank started cooking supper.

Name _____

Score _____

EXERCISE 10-4 Fragments in Paragraphs

On separate paper, rewrite the following short paragraphs to eliminate fragments.

1. Swahili is a Bantu language. Which is spoken by millions of people in Africa. It is written in a form of the Arabic alphabet. And, for the last hundred years, in the Roman alphabet.

2. Alfred Hitchcock was a famous movie director. Who was born and began his career in England. In addition to successful suspense movies such as *Rear Window, Vertigo,* and *The Birds.* Hitchcock also created two television series.

3. Although we usually think of snake venom as poisonous. The venoms of several snakes are used for medicinal purposes. Some venoms are useful in the treatment of diseases. Such as arthritis, asthma, and cancer.

4. Spending more time with hospitalized patients than doctors usually do. Nurses are often the first to notice problems or changes in a patient's condition. On the other hand, seeing a patient for perhaps only a few minutes a day. Doctors may not realize that an emotional problem is affecting a patient's physical recovery.

5. In Trivial Pursuit, an extremely popular board game. Players move around the board in a circle. Collecting colored wedges as they answer questions correctly. When a player has collected six wedges. He or she can move into the center.

EXERCISE 10-5 | Fragments in Paragraphs

On separate paper, rewrite the following short paragraphs to eliminate fragments.

1. Carol and Ed moved to Australia. A year after their marriage. Shortly before their first child was born. Decided to come back to the United States. So that they could be closer to their relatives.

2. The Religious Society of Friends the original name of the Quakers. A religion which began in England in the 17th century. Many Quakers settled in America under the leadership of William Penn. In the area of the country now known as Pennsylvania.

3. Learning English as a second language is not easy. Because English is not entirely phonetic. A letter might not have only one pronunciation. But might be pronounced several ways. The letter *a* has a different pronunciation. In each of these words—*hat, father,* and *made.*

4. The famous outlaw Jesse James born in Missouri in 1847. He and his brother Frank led a gang that robbed banks and held up trains. Tempted by a reward offered by the governor of Missouri. A gang member killed James in 1882.

5. Sri Lanka, a nation that was once called Ceylon. Is an island southeast of India. The island has had a history of invasions. Beginning in the sixth century B.C. with the Sinhalese. Other conquerors have included Tamils, the Dutch. And in 1795 the British.

11 Comma Splices and Fused Sentences

If two complete sentences are written as though they were one sentence, the result is a **run-on sentence.** The run-on is a **fused sentence** when there is no punctuation between the two independent clauses. The run-on is a **comma splice** when the two independent clauses are separated by only a comma. Run-ons can be corrected either by separating the two independent clauses with appropriate punctuation or by connecting the two independent clauses with a conjunction. Following are some examples.

The following fused sentence can be fixed by putting a period at the end of the first complete sentence and capitalizing the first word of the second complete sentence.

NOT: That day-care center is open from seven in the morning until seven at night these hours are convenient for working parents.

BUT: That day-care center is open from seven in the morning until seven at night. These hours are convenient for working parents.

The following comma splice can be corrected by separating the two complete sentences with a semicolon.

NOT: Huge pumpkins are usually not good for eating, however, they do make fine Jack O'Lanterns at Halloween.

BUT: Huge pumpkins are usually not good for eating; however, they do make fine Jack O'Lanterns at Halloween.

The following fused sentence can be corrected by connecting the two complete sentences with a comma and a coordinating conjunction.

NOT: During the storm the windows rattled the wind whistled in the chimney.

BUT: During the storm the windows rattled, **and** the wind whistled in the chimney.

The following comma splice can be fixed by using a subordinating conjunction to make one of the independent clauses into a dependent clause.

NOT: Going to a performance at the Fenice Theater in Venice, Italy can be a frustrating experience, some of the seats are behind pillars.

BUT: Going to a performance at the Fenice Theater in Venice, Italy can be a frustrating experience **because** some of the seats are behind pillars.

(See Exercises 11-1 through 11-8.)

EXERCISE 11-1   Run-ons

On separate paper, rewrite the following items to eliminate run-on sentences. One sentence has no run-ons.

> ***Example:***   He wanted to get his driver's license, he was too young.
>
> *He wanted to get his driver's license, but he was too young.*

1. Animals can be more than pets, dogs and some types of monkeys can be trained to help handicapped people.

2. Martin Luther King, Jr., is known primarily as a civil rights leader he was also an excellent writer.

3. Some people work well under pressure others do best in a quiet, stress-free environment.

4. Running shoes should be used only for running wearing them for other sports such as tennis or basketball could lead to serious injuries.

5. The college learning center once had only film strips and audiotapes; it recently added computers and software to its learning resources.

6. Four-year-old children are naturally curious, they constantly ask their parents questions.

7. Meat and dairy products provide complete protein, most vegetable proteins are incomplete.

8. *A Christmas Carol* by Charles Dickens has been made into several movies there are also some cartoon versions.

9. Compared to rice, bread is an expensive food it must be baked in an oven rather than cooked over a flame.

10. Copyright laws originally applied to written works, now the copyright laws cover music, films, and computer software.

EXERCISE 11-2   Run-ons

On separate paper, rewrite the following items to eliminate run-ons.

> **Example:**   Curtains hold in the heat they also keep the sun from fad-
> ing the furniture.
>
> *Curtains hold in the heat; they also keep the sun*
> *from fading the furniture.*

1. Four-wheel drive vehicles get worse gas mileage than two-wheel drive vehicles, four-wheel drive, on the other hand, provides better traction.

2. Christmas trees should not be allowed to dry out dry trees are a fire hazard.

3. Without carpeting, the offices would echo carpeting cuts down the noise.

4. One way to become a good speller is to read seeing words often fixes their
   spelling in the mind.

5. Mark retired last January, he plans to travel and to do volunteer work.

6. The student newspaper is good, however, it needs a better sports section.

7. Weight training increases an athlete's strength, aerobic exercise improves
   stamina.

8. Many holidays are clustered together, Columbus Day, Veterans Day,
   Thanksgiving, Christmas, Hanukkah, and New Year's Day all occur within
   three months.

9. Unprocessed foods are often more nutritious than processed foods, they are
   usually less expensive, too.

10. Fruit flies multiply quickly they are therefore useful for scientific study and
    experimentation.

EXERCISE 11-3   Run-ons

On separate paper, rewrite the following items to eliminate run-ons. One sentence has no run-ons.

> ***Example:***   She is eighty years old, she plays golf every day.
>
> *Even though she is eighty years old, she plays golf every day.*

1. The park is full of joggers at any hour one can see runners of all ages.

2. Instead of concentrating on a writer's work, sometimes the public focuses on the writer's private life.

3. Mail carriers know when the holidays are coming, they have to deliver countless heavy shopping catalogues.

4. Answering machines can be irritating, however, they are quite useful.

5. Annual plants die after one season, perennials do not.

6. Slide rules are not used much these days calculators have taken their place.

7. The sky clouded over in the morning, by noon it was raining.

8. This table has two extra leaves, when they are inserted, the table can seat twelve people.

9. Computers have made new kinds of furniture necessary once there was no need for computer and printer stands.

10. Hockey players need both strength and speed either one alone is not enough.

EXERCISE 11-4 | Run-ons in Paragraphs

On separate paper, rewrite the following paragraphs to eliminate run-ons. Not every sentence in each paragraph is a run-on.

1. The dancer and choreographer George Balanchine was born in Russia in 1904, he moved to America in 1933 and later became director of the New York City Ballet. He choreographed many works, most of which stress pure dance rather than tell a story.

2. Dozens of famous sayings are drawn from Shakespeare's plays many people who have not read the plays are familiar with the quotations. "A rose by any other name would smell as sweet" is an example, it is a line from *Romeo and Juliet*.

3. A prime number is an integer that can be divided only by 1 and itself the first five prime numbers are 2, 3, 5, 7, and 11. A number that has other divisors is not prime, it is called a composite number.

4. Every few years there are dire predictions about the movie industry. It was thought that television would replace movies the same thing was said after the advent of cable television. People said VCRs would be the final blow to movies, in fact, since the invention of the VCR, more, not fewer, movies are being made.

5. Apartments in recently constructed buildings have less space than older apartments, therefore, furniture that has a dual purpose is useful. Examples are sofas that convert to beds, also, beds can be designed with drawers and storage space underneath.

EXERCISE 11-5 | Run-ons in Paragraphs

On separate paper, rewrite the following paragraphs to eliminate run-ons. Not every sentence in each paragraph is a run-on.

1. Condominium and cooperative apartments offer different arrangements to buyers. People who buy a co-op are not buying the actual apartment, they are buying shares in the apartment building. Condominiums are different, their owners own the actual apartment.

2. Japanese netsuke are small knobs carved out of wood, ivory, or other materials. These objects were originally made as ornaments on sashes or girdles, they are so beautifully made that art collectors became interested in them.

3. Children's advocates have criticized certain recent television programs these shows, most of which are cartoons, feature characters that were first created as toys. The shows might entertain children, however, the programs can be considered extended advertisements for commercial products.

4. Advances in science and technology sometimes eliminate the need for certain kinds of medical treatment, one example is the treatment of tuberculosis. Years ago there were hundreds of tuberculosis sanitariums they are no longer necessary because of modern drugs and improved public sanitation.

5. The work *epistle* means letter, a novel in the epistolary style tells the story through letters written by the novel's characters. The central character of *The Color Purple* by Alice Walker writes letters to her sister the letters chronicle the difficulties and pain of her life.

EXERCISE 11-6   Fragments and Run-ons

On separate paper, rewrite the following brief paragraphs to eliminate fragments and run-ons.

1. The Nile the longest river in the world, over four thousand miles. It rises in central Africa and flows northward to the Mediterranean Sea, it drains over one million square miles, about one-tenth of Africa.

2. Although whales never leave the water. They are mammals that are warm-blooded and feed their young with milk. Some whales have teeth, others have baleen but no teeth. The latter use their baleen to strain water from their food.

3. Unlike movies, which are filmed in small segments, a play is performed in two or three hours straight. Therefore, actors who work in the theater must have stamina, without stamina they could never do eight shows a week. Usually six evening performances and two matinees.

4. Years ago, tennis rules stated that a player must win a set by two games, now when the score in a set is even at six games, a tie-breaker is played. The tie-breaker put an end to matches lasting all day. Thereby making tennis easier to televise.

5. Charles Dodgson taught mathematics at Oxford University for more than twenty-five years, although he wrote a book about the mathematician Euclid, he is better known for *Alice's Adventures in Wonderland* and *Through the Looking Glass*. Which he wrote under the pen name of Lewis Carroll.

EXERCISE 11-7 | Fragments and Run-ons

On separate paper, rewrite the following brief paragraphs to eliminate fragments and run-ons.

1. The book *Blue Highways* was written by William Least Heat Moon. Who traveled throughout America, visiting small towns and meeting people. He did not use major highways, instead, he deliberately chose smaller roads that in atlases are colored blue.

2. The Cloisters is a branch of the Metropolitan Museum of Art, located in upper Manhattan, it is a museum specializing in medieval art. Among its famous holdings is the series of tapestries. Called "The Hunt of the Unicorn."

3. Instructional videotapes now a booming business. In addition to videotapes of movies, consumers can buy or rent videos that teach. Tapes of exercise and cooking classes are common people can also get videos about gardening, home repair, and financial planning.

4. Many people who love living in the city. Do not like high-rise apartment buildings. They claim such buildings do not create a sense of community. There are too many tenants to be able to get to know one's neighbors, also it is impossible to keep an eye on one's children playing outside.

5. The social critic Thorstein Veblen wrote, among other books, *The Theory of the Leisure Class,* he also coined the phrase "conspicuous consumption." He noted that certain items of dress were not useful. But instead were a proclamation of wealth.

EXERCISE 11-8   Sentence Completions

Complete each sentence by adding to the given words. Make sure your finished sentence is neither a fragment nor a run-on.

1. After reading the morning newspaper, _____

   _____ .

2. _____

   _____ although he had not spoken Swahili in many years.

3. The library is open six days a week, and _____

   _____ .

4. Although Mozart was only in his thirties when he died, _____

   _____ .

5. When I first came to this college, _____

   _____ .

6. _____ in order to prepare
   for the state boards in nursing.

7. _____ , yet some people feel
   more relaxed after drinking a cup of coffee.

8. Dictionaries provide more than spelling and syllabification; _____

   _____ .

9. _____ , which
   was advertised on radio and television.

10. As soon as the temperature fell to 32 degrees, _____

    _____ .

12 Verb Forms

12a Present Infinitive, Past Tense, Past Participle, and Present Participle

English verbs have four principal parts or forms: the **present infinitive, past tense, past participle,** and **present participle.** Here are some examples.

PRESENT INFINITIVE	PAST TENSE	PAST PARTICIPLE	PRESENT PARTICIPLE
drink	drank	drunk	drinking
pay	paid	paid	paying
ring	rang	rung	ringing
speak	spoke	spoken	speaking
teach	taught	taught	teaching
play	played	played	playing
receive	received	received	receiving
study	studied	studied	studying
walk	walked	walked	walking

Regular verbs add *-ed* or *-d* to form the past tense and the past participle. *Irregular verbs* show the past tense and past participle with spelling changes. For example, the verb *ring* does not add "ed" to form the past tense and the past participle; instead, the spelling changes to *rang* for past tense and to *rung* for the past participle. If you are unsure of the verb form, use your dictionary, which lists the four principal forms of verbs. (See Exercises 12-1 to 12-6.)

12b Troublesome Verbs

Using the *-ed* ending correctly

Sometimes students omit necessary *-ed* endings because they believe that the *-ed* is needed only for the past tense. The *-ed* is also used at the end of regular verbs when the verb phrase contains a form of the verb *to have* or *to be* or another verb of being.

FORMS OF TO HAVE	FORMS OF TO BE		VERBS OF BEING
have	am	were	seem
has	is	be	feel
had	are	being	appear
having	was	been	become
			look

The following examples are *not* in the past tense; each *-ed* ending is necessary because one of the words in the preceding list appears in the verb phrase.

You should **have** call**ed** me.
He **is** not satisfi**ed** with the results.
We **felt** exhaust**ed.**

If the verb phrase does not contain one of the words listed, the *-ed* ending is not needed. (See Exercise 12-7.)

EXERCISE 12-1 Verb Forms

Choose the correct verb form. If necessary, use your dictionary.

> ***Example:*** The committee's report will be (~~distribute~~, distributed) today.

1. The project has been (*finish, finished*).

2. The jury (*took, taken*) three days to reach a verdict.

3. She has (*ran, run*) in two marathons.

4. Last night his car was (*stole, stolen*).

5. I (*saw, seen*) the ballet *Swan Lake* last night.

6. We have (*saw, seen*) that movie twice.

7. Rembrandt (*drew, drawn*) preliminary sketches for his paintings.

8. They'd (*ate, eaten*) dinner early that night.

9. We had not met in years, but I (*knew, known*) him at once.

10. He's (*chose, chosen*) to major in political science.

EXERCISE 12-2   Verb Forms

Choose the correct verb form.

> ***Example:***   People on the block had (~~came~~, (come)) to welcome their new neighbors.

1. A meter reader had (*came, come*) to the door.

2. When the bell (*rang, rung*), classes (*began, begun*).

3. Several books had (*fell, fallen*) off the shelves.

4. No one liked passing the garbage dump because it (*stank, stunk*).

5. Mr. and Mrs. Han have (*decide, decided*) to start their own catering business.

6. She (*saw, seen*) the movie last night for the first time; I have (*saw, seen*) it twice already.

7. During her pregnancy, she (*drank, drunk*) a quart of milk a day.

8. When the car overturned, the passengers were (*threw, thrown*) out.

9. The whistle (*blew, blown*) every day at noon.

10. This time he's (*went, gone*) too far!

EXERCISE 12-3 Verb Forms

Choose the correct verb form.

> ***Example:*** The work will be (~~finish~~, (finished)) next week.

1. Henry Aaron (*broke, broken*) Babe Ruth's home-run record.

2. The high school chorus (*sang, sung*) Verdi's *Requiem*.

3. This witness has (*swore, sworn*) to tell the truth.

4. The constant noise (*drove, driven*) me crazy.

5. When the quarterback was (*tackle, tackled*), his jersey (*tore, torn*).

6. You've (*gave, given*) away the plot of the movie.

7. That's all she (*wrote, written*).

8. The sweater (*shrank, shrunk*) in the wash.

9. The concert has not (*began, begun*) yet.

10. Plants in that poor soil have not (*grew, grown*) well.

EXERCISE 12-4   Verb Forms

Choose the correct verb forms.

1. When the gymnasium was being (*build, built*), an enormous excavation was (*dig, dug*) for the basement. Digging (*took, taken*) two weeks before the foundation could be poured.

2. Because Peter (*knew, known*) he needed to lose weight, he (*chose, chosen*) a sensible exercise program. For the past year, he has (*swam, swum*) a mile three times a week.

3. People who have (*drank, drunk*) too much and then have (*drove, driven*) their cars have endangered both themselves and others. Such people should be (*gave, given*) jail sentences.

4. First, Joe mended any clothing that was (*tore, torn*). He then (*did, done*) two load of laundry. Later, he discovered that several of his shirts had (*shrank, shrunk*) in the wash.

5. Sara (*think, thought*) that she (*saw, seen*) the person who had (*stole, stolen*) her bike. She (*ran, run*) after him, but he jumped over a fence and (*got, gotten*) away.

6. Ms. Ragin (*become, became*) interested in teaching when she (*took, taken*) a course in early childhood education. Before that time, she had not (*knew, known*) what career she wanted.

7. Chi Yun (*threw, thrown*) a large stack of letters onto her desk. Later, when she (*began, begun*) to open them, she noticed that some of the envelopes were (*tore, torn*).

8. Herbert (*wrote, written*) an article about his childhood in the country. He described a pond where he and his brothers had (*swam, swum*) in the summer and had skated in winter when the water (*froze, frozen*).

9. The subway conductor (*gave, given*) directions to the passengers, but the loudspeaker was (*broke, broken*), so nobody (*understand, understood*).

10. After discovering that he had (*drove, driven*) the wrong way, Ron asked for directions. He (*spoke, spoken*) to a police officer, who (*drew, drawn*) him a little map.

Name _____

Score _____

Replace each inappropriate verb form with the appropriate form.

>   written
> **Example:**   He had not ~~wrote~~ the letter.

1. The frightened children clinged to their mother.

2. The television program *M.A.S.H.* run for eleven years.

3. I have never rode on a rollercoaster.

4. The boy runned too fast, falled down, and hurt himself.

5. All of the students had went to the seminar.

6. The nursing instructor teached a lesson on I.V. regulation.

7. The *Titanic* had sank in the Atlantic Ocean.

8. I was shook when the phone rang unexpectedly.

9. A traffic helicopter flown above the crowded highway.

10. He flinged off his coat and throwed himself into a chair.

EXERCISE 12-6   Writing with Specified Verbs

For each item, write a short paragraph using the suggested verbs and phrases. Use separate paper.

1. planted, had dug, spread

2. stank, swam, tore

3. had crept, flung, he was caught

4. they have known, had come, it was lost

5. she has spoken, stung, it has taught

6. had chosen, had forgotten, had known

7. grew, kept, took

8. wrote, spoke, swore

9. had rung, had risen, had quit

10. drank, began, gave

EXERCISE 12-7 | Testing *-ed* Verb Forms

Choose the correct verb form.

> ***Example:*** At the moment he feels (~~exhaust~~, (exhausted)).

1. Dr. Ruiz was (*elate, elated*) when his article was (*publish, published*).

2. I was (*infuriate, infuriated*) because the phone did not (*work, worked*).

3. They will (*graduate, graduated*) from college next spring.

4. By next summer, Ms. Woods will have (*graduate, graduated*) from college.

5. The floors are being (*wash, washed*) and (*wax, waxed*).

6. Ms. Shen has (*decide, decided*) to major in history.

7. He seems (*worry, worried*); perhaps we should (*ask, asked*) if he is all right.

8. The window had been (*smash, smashed*).

9. He should have (*remember, remembered*) to lock the office.

10. The doctor's records show that the children were (*immunize, immunized*) last year.

13 Subject–Verb Agreement

A verb must agree in number with its subject. A singular subject needs a singular verb form, and a plural subject needs a plural verb form.

In the present tense, all verbs, (except *be* and *have*) add *-s* or *-es* in the third-person singular. Therefore, if a subject is **he, she, it,** or a singular word, the present tense verb ends in *-s* (and *have* changes to *has*). Here are some examples.

The dog barks.

The subject *dog* is third-person singular, so the verb *barks* ends in *-s*.

The dogs bark.

The subject *dogs* is plural, so there is no *-s* added to the verb.

The verb *to be* has irregular forms in the present and past tenses.

PRESENT TENSE		PAST TENSE	
I am	we are	I was	we were
you are	you are	you were	you were
he/she/it is	they are	he/she/it was	they were

13a Compound Subjects

A **compound subject** with the word *and* usually takes a plural verb form. When a compound subject has the word *or* or *nor*, the verb agrees with the closer part of the subject. Here are some examples.

Alice and Marge are good friends.

The plural verb *are* agrees with the compound subject *Alice and Marge*.

Neither the girls nor Jack is wearing a coat.

The singular verb *is* agrees with *Jack,* the closer part of the subject.

Either Jack or the girls have to wash the car.

The plural verb *have* agrees with *girls,* the closer part of the subject.

13b Intervening Phrases and Clauses

Often, phrases and clauses separate subjects and verbs. The verb must agree with its subject, not with a word in the intervening phrase or clause. In the following examples, parentheses surround words intervening between subjects and verbs.

Some **students** (in the class) **have read** that book.
Her **humor,** (as well as her kindness), **makes** her popular.
One (of these shoes) **needs** a new sole.
The **customers** (who complained about shoddy merchandise) **are getting** refunds.
Paula, (who was hired as a temporary worker), **is being offered** a permanent job.

13c Collective Nouns

Some subjects create difficulty because they "feel" plural, yet they are actually singular. For example, a **collective noun** refers to a group of people or things as a single unit, so the collective noun takes a singular verb. Some often-used collective nouns are *army, committee, family, group, jury, team.*

The **jury is** in the courtroom.
Her **family gets** together at Thanksgiving.
The **team has** not yet lost a game.

13d Nouns Plural in Form but Singular in Meaning

Some words look plural but are singular in meaning, and they therefore take singular verbs. Some common words in this category are *checkers, civics, economics, mathematics, measles, molasses, mumps, news, physics, statistics.*

Molasses pours slowly.
Checkers is a deceptively simple game.

13e Indefinite and Relative Pronouns

Indefinite pronouns and words ending in *-one, -body,* and *-thing* are singular and need singular verbs.

Nobody knows the answer.
Everyone needs food, clothing, and shelter.
Everything is in its place.

When the subject is a relative pronoun (*who, that,* or *which*), the verb must agree with the pronoun's antecedent.

People **who exercise** regularly reduce health problems. (*plural antecedent*)

The announcer **who comes** on at 8 a.m. has a pleasant voice. (*singular antecedent*)

Cars **that have** front-wheel drive handle snowy conditions well. (*plural antecedent*)

The bus **that stops** here is an express. (*singular antecedent*)

This book, **which was** first published in 1920, is now out of print. (*singular antecedent*)

Those stores, **which are** all located on the same block, have hired a private guard. (*plural antecedent*)

Some words may be singular or plural, depending on other words in the sentence.

All of the money **is** gone. (*singular*)
All of the pennies **are** gone. (*plural*)

13f Titles

A subject that is a title takes a singular verb, even if the title contains plural words.

***Flowers in the Attic* is** a frightening book.
***The Canterbury Tales* was** written centuries ago.
"The Windows" **is** a poem by George Herbert.

13g Units of Measurement, Time, and Money

A subject that is a unit of measurement, time, or money takes a singular verb.

Six miles is his usual run every morning.
Five minutes is not enough time to exercise properly.
Ten dollars is too expensive for a movie ticket.

13h Inverted Sentence Order

A verb must agree with its subject even if the subject follows the verb. Words such as *there* and *here* are never the subject. The words *here* and *there* are adverbs and therefore cannot be the subject of a sentence.

There **is** a **squirrel** running across the road.
Hanging on the wall **are** her **diplomas.**
Here **is** the **book** you asked me to find.
Outside the arena **was** a huge **crowd.**
There **are** two **candidates** for the job.

13i Agreement with Subject, Not Predicate Nominative

If the subject and the predicate nominative differ in number, the verb should agree with the subject.

His worst **fear is** rats.
Car **seatbelts are** an important safety feature.
This gymnast's best **event is** the rings.

13j Gerunds as Subjects

A **gerund** is a verb form ending in *-ing* and used as a noun in a sentence. A gerund is the name of one single activity, and, therefore, when the gerund is a subject, it takes a singular verb.

Walking *is* good exercise.
Exercising *has* helped them lose weight.

A **gerund phrase,** consisting of a gerund and all its complements and modifiers, can also be the subject of a sentence. The gerund phrase as a subject is singular and therefore takes a singular verb, even if the gerund's complements are plural.

Cooking some kinds of beans *takes* a long time.
Wearing the latest fashions *is* important to them.

(See Exercises 13-1 through 13-14.)

Name _____

Score _____

EXERCISE 13-1   Subjects and Verbs

Write *S* over the subject and *V* over the verb in each of the following sentences.

> $\overset{\text{S}}{}\quad\overset{\text{V}}{}$
>
> ***Example:***   The meeting lasted for twenty minutes.

1. Many people meet in the park for lunch on sunny days.

2. After her nap, the baby wants some attention.

3. The garden's best feature is the rosebushes.

4. The delayed commuters were anxious and tired.

5. The wrestling team was in the division finals.

6. These books are due in two weeks.

7. Customers often compare prices before buying an item.

8. This customer always compares prices before buying an item.

9. Some bees signal the location of honey by a sort of dance in the air.

10. The main ingredient of marmalade is oranges.

Name _____

Score _____

EXERCISE 13-2 Subjects and Verbs

Write *S* over the subject and *V* over the verb in each sentence. Cross out any phrases and clauses that intervene between subject and verb.

>   S   V
> **Example:**   Two people ~~in the class~~ are from Haiti.

1. Nureyev and Baryshnikov are both originally from the Soviet Union.

2. One of the headlights is broken.

3. The dog, not counting his collar, leash, and tags, weighs 80 pounds.

4. Either prunes or liver is a good source of iron.

5. Neither the phone nor the electricity is working after the storm this morning.

6. The members of the jury were listening intently to the witness.

7. Sam Shepard, a well-known actor, is also a playwright.

8. Hannah and Abigail are biblical names.

9. Two slices of this pie have been eaten.

10. Michelle, who is eleven years old, wants to be a ballet dancer.

EXERCISE 13-3   Subjects and Verbs

Write *S* over the subject and *V* over the verb in each sentence.

> S   V
> ***Example:***   Nobody knows her name.

1. Mumps is a contagious disease.

2. His family has a reunion every summer.

3. Almost everybody uses public transportation.

4. Most of these dollar bills are new.

5. Most of the money has been collected.

6. Forty minutes is not enough time to discuss the issue thoroughly.

7. Physics is her favorite subject.

8. Everyone keeps glancing at the clock.

9. The jury was sent out of the room.

10. *The Simpsons* is a popular television show.

EXERCISE 13-4   Relative Pronouns and Verbs

Write *S* over each relative pronoun (*who, which, that*) and *V* over its verb. Draw an arrow from the relative pronoun to its antecedent.

> **Example:** Salads that are covered in oil are not low calorie.
> S V

1. Any person who wants a copy of this article should ask for one.

2. The car that was parked outside the house is gone now.

3. This dress, which is one hundred years old, belonged to my great-grand-mother.

4. The files that were misplaced have been located.

5. Helima's poetry, which has been published in several magazines, is hard to understand.

6. *Paradise Lost,* which was written by John Milton, describes the fall of Adam and Eve.

7. Those tenants, who want improvements made, are holding a meeting.

8. Any employees who have suggestions should put them in the box.

9. Foods that are filled with empty calories are not nutritious.

10. Everybody who works on that floor has a large office.

EXERCISE 13-5 Subjects and Verbs in Inverted Sentences

Write *S* over the subject and *V* over the verb in each sentence.

>   V   S
> **Example:**   There are two trucks in the driveway.

1. Sulking in his tent was Achilles.

2. Over the bookshelf there is a mirror.

3. Here are two copies of your lease.

4. There are no people in the lobby.

5. Between the windows hangs an oil painting.

6. There were two fire engines racing down the street.

7. Behind the door stands a coatrack.

8. At the end of the book is the index.

9. Here are the trophies won by the track team.

10. There is an interesting article on page 53.

EXERCISE 13-6   Subject–Verb Agreement

Revise any sentence in which a verb does not agree with its subject. One sentence is correct as written.

> *Example:*   Testing all those recipes ~~are~~ ^{is} time consuming.

1. Mary Garcia hope to get into law school.

2. The fruits and vegetables was arranged in piles.

3. Either the train or the bus are a convenient way to get to work.

4. One of these people have to use the telephone.

5. Our baseball team are scheduled to play thirty games.

6. Everybody have ways of fighting boredom.

7. *Cats* are a show based on poems by T. S. Eliot.

8. There is three photos of the governor on the front page of the newspaper.

9. Rearranging all these shelves are your first job.

10. Great Britain, unlike New England, does not get extremely cold in the winter.

EXERCISE 13-7 | Subject–Verb Agreement

Revise any sentence in which a verb does not agree with its subject. One sentence is correct as written.

> **Example:** There ~~wasn't~~ weren't any people in the room.

1. Neither he nor his wife have been to Mexico.

2. The seats in this waiting room is not comfortable.

3. Living in a big family with many relatives were an impossible dream.

4. Five years seem like a short sentence for kidnapping.

5. In the lower right corner of the painting are the artist's signature.

6. This clock, which keep perfect time, is one hundred years old.

7. Peas and beans helps to fix nitrogen in the garden soil.

8. A compass, a protractor, and a calculator are on my shopping list.

9. These windshield wipers needs to be replaced.

10. The committee want to meet again this afternoon.

EXERCISE 13-8   Subject–Verb Agreement

Revise any sentence in which a verb does not agree with its subject. One sentence is correct as written.

> ***Example:***   Everybody ~~have~~ has to take history.

1. The committee meet every Monday in the conference room.

2. One hundred yards are the length of an American football field.

3. There are not any reason to worry about your health.

4. The look in her eyes were easy to understand.

5. Several people was waiting for the pharmacy to open.

6. Barbara Jordan, who were a member of Congress, is an excellent speaker.

7. Here are the office supplies you ordered.

8. Everyone hope that it will be a mild winter.

9. Either the scouts or the leader were supposed to bring the maps.

10. Chickens and ducks was running all over the barnyard.

EXERCISE 13-9 | Subject–Verb Agreement

Revise any sentence in which a verb does not agree with its subject. One sentence is correct as written.

> **Example:**   He is meeting with the new people who ~~was~~ hired.
>   *were*

1. In the library, nobody were talking.

2. Two dollars and fifty cents were all the money I had left.

3. Her dedication, as well as her hard work, deserve recognition.

4. José's family live in Boston.

5. Ten miles is too long a run for a beginner to attempt.

6. Caring for many patients aren't easy.

7. The computers that is featured in the advertisement have color monitors.

8. Ann and Carol has been good friends since their college days.

9. Sitting on the front steps was three children.

10. Neither Tom nor Niv want to walk the dog.

Name _____

Score _____

EXERCISE 13-10   Subject–Verb Agreement in Paragraphs

In the following brief paragraphs, revise any sentences in which a verb does not agree with its subject. Not every sentence has a subject–verb error. Use separate paper.

1. The mysteries written by Dick Francis is fun, though they certainly is not great literature. Francis was once a jockey, and many of his characters is jockeys, horse trainers, owners, and racecourse stewards.

2. Many people does not realize that the most important piece of clothing in winter is a hat. A large percentage of the heat loss people experience are through the head. Wearing a hat cuts the heat loss considerably.

3. Everybody who read newspapers are familiar with the drawings of courtroom artists. Judges, lawyers, witnesses, and the jury is drawn by artists sitting in the courtroom. The introduction of cameras into courtrooms are sure to affect the livelihood of these artists.

4. Quilted works of art and stained glass is alike in some respects, for both the choice and the placement of color are important. There are one important difference—stained glass breaks, but quilts does not.

5. There is many versions of the fairy tale "Cinderella." The story of the poor girl who becomes a princess is told all over the world, though the details varies. In the English tale, the girl drop a glass slipper; in the Vietnamese version, the slippers is embroidered with silk.

EXERCISE 13-11 Subject–Verb Agreement in Paragraphs

In the following brief paragraphs, revise any sentences in which a verb does not agree with its subject. Not every sentence has a subject-verb error. Use separate paper.

1. Some people prefer artificial Christmas trees because they does not dry out and because there are just a one-time expense. On the other hand, people who always buy live trees says that their color and their fragrance is far superior to those of artificial trees.

2. The life of Miguel de Cervantes, the author of *Don Quixote de la Mancha,* were almost as exciting as the fantasies of his fictional character, Don Quixote himself. Among other episodes was enlistment in the army, a crippling war wound, capture by pirates, and five years of slavery.

3. An "artificial tongue" is a language that have not developed naturally, but are created by people who uses elements from natural languages. One example of artificial languages is Esperanto, which were invented in the 19th century by Dr. Ludwig L. Zamenhof of Poland.

4. In the Scrovegni chapel in the Italian city of Padua, there is thirty-eight frescoes painted by Giotto. These frescoes show scenes from the Last Judgment and from the lives of Mary and Jesus. Many critics considers Giotto's paintings to be among the greatest works of Italian art.

5. Many people believes that Abner Doubleday invented baseball, but that report is disputed. Alexander Cartwright and Henry Chadwick was equally important to the development of the game. In any case, baseball certainly are regarded as America's national game.

EXERCISE 13-12 Sentence Completions with Verbs

Complete each sentence. Make sure the subjects and verbs agree.

1. Mr. and Mrs. Gowie, who live in Iowa, (*verb*) _____

_____

2. All of her children (*verb*) _____

_____

3. All of my money (*verb*) _____

_____

4. Everybody who is enrolled at the college (*verb*) _____

_____

5. One hundred years (*verb*) _____

_____

6. The girls' lacrosse team (*verb*) _____

_____

7. My family (*verb*) _____

_____

8. Neither the bus nor the subway (*verb*) _____

_____

9. There are (*subject*) _____

_____

10. Several of these pencils (*verb*) _____

_____

Name _____

Score _____

EXERCISE 13-13 Sentence Completions with Verbs

Complete each sentence. Make sure the subjects and verbs agree.

1. Here is (*subject*) _____

   _____

2. Either Mr. Ray or Mr. Chin (*verb*) _____

   _____

3. There was (*subject*) _____

   _____

4. The Knicks and Celtics (*verb*) _____

   _____

5. This clothing, along with some shoes, (*verb*) ____

   _____

6. The guide leading a large group of tourists (*verb*) ___

   _____

7. Anybody who (*verb*) _____

   _____

8. The person who (*verb*) _____

   _____

9. The coffee in those cups (*verb*) _____

   _____

10 Throughout the United States, everybody (*verb*) ___

   _____

EXERCISE 13-14 Writing Paragraphs in Specified Verb Tenses

On separate paper, write a brief paragraph for each of the following topics using the tense specified.

1. Describe a classroom. Use only the *present tense*.

2. Describe an event that happened to *one* of your relatives in the past. Use the *past tense*.

3. Write a description of how *one* of your friends studies. Write in the *present tense*.

4. Choose a married couple with children, and describe how they handle their children in a difficult situation. Use the *present tense* wherever possible.

5. Write a description of how you think an ideal friend behaves. As much as you can, use the *present tense*.

14 Pronouns: Agreement, Reference, and Usage

14a Pronoun–Antecedent Agreement

Pronouns must agree with their antecedents (the words to which they refer) in number and gender.

> *Dr. Wright* checked to see if **she** had all **her** notes for **her** lecture. (She *and* her *are singular, feminine pronouns that agree with the antecedent* Dr. Wright.)
>
> Several *customers* wanted **their** money back. (Their *is a plural pronoun agreeing with the antecedent* customers.)

Indefinite pronouns as antecedents

Sometimes an **indefinite pronoun** refers to a specifically masculine or feminine antecedent, and therefore the choice of pronoun is clear.

> There are eight women on the gymnastics team. *Each* has **her** own style.

Sometimes indefinite singular pronouns such as *everyone* and *everybody* refer to groups including both men and women. The word *everybody* is singular, so pronouns referring to it should also be singular. In the past, the masculine pronoun *his* was used to refer to an antecedent including both men and women. Today this usage is considered sexist and *his or her* is preferred.

> *Everybody* is entitled to **his or her** opinion.

To avoid repeating *his or her* many times, you can reword the sentence or change to the plural.

> Everybody is entitled to an opinion.
> All people are entitled to their opinions.

Using plural antecedents such as *all people, people in general, most parents, many students,* and so on both avoids the problem of sexist language and makes the agreement of antecedent, subject and verb, and pronoun logical and simple.

Relative pronouns

The **relative pronouns** *who, whom,* and *whose* usually refer to people; *that* and *which* refer to things and animals. *What* is not a relative pronoun.

> The salesperson **whom** you hired is doing an excellent job.
> The woman **whose** wallet you found is very grateful.
> The class **that** I am taking meets at 3 p.m.

The antecedent of a relative pronoun determines whether other pronouns should be singular or plural.

> *Ruth,* **who** is showing **her** paintings at the art gallery, is a professor of art.
> *Commuters* **who** drive **their** cars to work often face long traffic delays.

Pronouns and compound antecedents

A plural pronoun agrees with a **compound antecedent** joined by *and.* When the antecedent is a compound joined by *or, nor, neither/nor, either/or,* or *not only/but also,* the pronoun should agree with the nearer part of the compound.

> *Ron and Miguel* have resolved **their** differences.
> Neither the city councillors nor the *mayor* wanted to make public **her** views on the tax hike.

Pronouns and collective nouns

A **collective noun** names a group that is one unit, even though the unit may have many members. A singular pronoun is used to refer to a collective noun antecedent.

> The *team* is proud of **its** winning record.
> The financial *committee* will give **its** report at the next meeting.

If the members of a group are thought of as individuals, a plural antecedent and a plural pronoun are used.

The *members* of the jury are looking at **their** watches.

(See Exercises 14-1 through 14-4.)

14b Pronoun Reference

A pronoun should refer to a clearly stated antecedent rather than refer vaguely to an entire sentence. A sentence containing a pronoun with a vague reference should be rewritten either to eliminate the pronoun or to provide a clear antecedent.

> VAGUE: Chairmaine reads aloud when she proofreads, **which** irritates her classmates.
>
> CLEAR: Chairmaine cannot proofread without reading aloud, a *habit* **that** irritates her classmates.

Ambiguous pronoun reference occurs when a pronoun could refer to more than one antecedent. A sentence with an ambiguous reference should be rewritten so that the reference is clear.

> AMBIGUOUS: Martha told Irma that **she** had received a raise.

It is unclear whether Martha or Irma received the raise. If *she* refers to Martha, the sentence can be rewritten as follows:

> CLEAR: Martha said to Irma, "I have been given a raise."
> CLEAR: Martha, who had been given a raise, told Irma the news.
> CLEAR: After Martha received a raise, she told Irma about it.

If the pronoun *she* refers to Irma, the sentence can be written as follows:

> CLEAR: Martha said to Irma, "You have been given a raise."
> CLEAR: Martha told Irma that Irma had received a raise.

(See Exercise 14-5.)

14c Pronoun Usage

A personal pronoun should never follow immediately after its antecedent.

> INCORRECT: The tourist **he** wanted directions to the Lincoln Memorial.
> CORRECT: The tourist wanted directions to the Lincoln Memorial.

A pronoun ending in *-self* or *-selves* is used only when the sentence contains an antecedent for the pronoun. The following is a list of all pronouns ending in *-self* or *-selves:*

myself	itself
yourself	ourselves
himself	yourselves
herself	themselves

CORRECT: The *Smiths* painted their house **themselves.**

INCORRECT: Joe sent copies of the letter to Irene and **myself.**

CORRECT: Joe sent copies of the letter to Irene and **me.**

(See Exercises 14-6 through 14-11.)

EXERCISE 14-1 Pronouns and Antecedents

Draw a line from the pronoun to its antecedent in each of the following sentences.

> *Example:* Mrs. Chan is in her office.

1. Roxanna parked her car in the driveway.

2. The passengers have fastened their seatbelts.

3. Each major league baseball manager has his own style of managing.

4. These employees want to know if they can change their schedules.

5. Howard walks his dog every morning at 7:30.

6. I would like to paint the kitchen myself.

7. These security guards have finished their shift.

8. The cashier is checking her register.

9. Every employee at this factory must carry his or her identification card.

10. Fidel rolled up the rug and carried it upstairs.

EXERCISE 14-2   Pronouns and Antecedents

Draw a line from the pronoun to its antecedent in each of the following sentences. Then rewrite each sentence to eliminate the phrase *his or her*.

Example: Every person should vote to make sure his or her voice is heard.

All people should vote to make sure their voices are heard.

---

1. Somebody has left his or her umbrella under a chair.

   _____

   _____

2. A parent ought to read to his or her young children every day.

   _____

   _____

3. Each student should choose a major in which he or she is truly interested.

   _____

   _____

4. Every citizen on this block has put his or her name on the petition.

   _____

   _____

5. Everybody in line was rubbing his or her hands and stamping his or her feet.

   _____

   _____

6. No one has completed his or her project yet.

   _____

   _____

7. Everyone wants a decent life for his or her family.

   _____

   _____

8. A teacher has to divide his or her time equally among all his or her students.

   _____

   _____

9. A nurse must observe his or her patients carefully.

   _____

   _____

10. Each homeowner is responsible for his or her property.

    _____

    _____

EXERCISE 14-3 Relative Pronouns and Antecedents

Draw a line from the relative pronoun to its antecedent in each of the following sentences. If a sentence has another pronoun, draw a line from it to the relative pronoun.

> *Example:* The college, which is celebrating its fortieth birthday, is located near all major transportation.

1. This highway, which was built in 1935, is too narrow for today's traffic.

2. Customers who want their money back must see the manager.

3. The boy whom Liz met at last night's party is on the phone.

4. The graduating student whose grades are highest in the class wins an academic award.

5. The books that Joe borrowed are on the desk.

6. Marie, whose parents are from Switzerland, speaks four languages.

7. The man whom you see at the far desk is an accountant.

8. The accident, which luckily caused no major damage, occurred last night.

9. The medicine that Dr. Ford prescribed tastes awful.

10. People who exercise regularly lose less time at work than people who do not.

Name _____

Score _____

Antecedents

Draw a line from the pronoun to its antecedent in each of the following sentences.

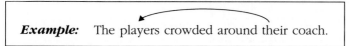

Example: The players crowded around their coach.

1. The soccer team plays its first game of the season tomorrow.

2. A police car and an ambulance were sounding their sirens.

3. Neither the coach nor the players would discuss their game plan.

4. Neither the players nor the coach would discuss his game plan.

5. All the members of the church choir have their hymnals.

6. The emergency rescue squad has been given its next assignment.

7. Both the catcher and the star relief pitcher want to renegotiate their contracts.

8. The hardware store is moving to a new location because it needs more space.

9. Either Tina or Angela can show the class how she solved the math problem.

10. Neither Mr. Brown nor Mr. Smith could hide his anger.

EXERCISE 14-5 | Pronoun Reference

Rewrite the following sentences to eliminate vague and ambiguous pronoun references.

> **Example:** He is very angry, which disturbs me.
>
> *His extreme anger disturbs me.*

1. If Mr. King hires Mr. Fields, he will be very happy.

   _____

   _____

2. Laura asked Liz if she could spend the night at her house.

   _____

   _____

3. Amira is a fine dancer, and she gets a lot of pleasure from this.

   _____

   _____

4. Mark was overwhelmed by the quiet and beauty of the mountains. It was an experience he would never forget.

   _____

   _____

5. Very cold weather and heavy snow can both damage trees, but it causes branches to break off and is therefore more serious.

   _____

   _____

6. Dr. Rohas met Dr. Green when she first came to University Hospital.

_____

_____

7. Nilsa dislikes crowds and noise. This makes her quite nervous.

_____

_____

8. The baby was quiet and seldom cried, which worried his parents.

_____

_____

9. Mr. Wright likes people to be candid and honest because this tells him where he stands with them.

_____

_____

10. Mr. Williams asked Mr. Lee to hold the meeting in his office.

_____

_____

EXERCISE 14-6   Pronoun Usage

Rewrite each sentence to eliminate pronoun usage problems. One sentence is correct as written.

> **Example:**   Andy he was the one who called myself.
>
> *Andy was the one who called me.*

1. Martha she was the one who built the bookcase.

_____

2. I knew that Mr. and Mrs. Diaz they wanted to find a bigger apartment.

_____

3. Please send your resume to myself.

_____

4. Mark Twain he wrote *The Adventures of Huckleberry Finn*.

_____

5. Nancy painted a picture of her sister Jean and herself.

_____

6. The letter was addressed only to herself, not to her husband.

_____

7. Bella Smith she witnessed the bank robbery.

_____

8. Copies of the book were sent to Professor Salgado and myself.

_____

9. Give your suggestions for scheduling improvements to myself or to Philip.

   _____

10. The sportscaster said that the Celtics they had traded two players.

   _____

EXERCISE 14-7 Pronoun Agreement, Reference, and Usage

Rewrite the following sentences to eliminate pronoun agreement, reference, and usage problems. One sentence is correct as written.

> **Example:** Each person must make up their own mind about the issue.
>
> *Each person must make up his or her own mind about the issue.*

1. There are ten girls in the class. Each one has designed their own science project.

   _____

2. Ms. Bell and Ms. McGee have finished her assignments.

   _____

3. The washing machine what the Bromleys own is old, but it still works well.

   _____

4. Marie Curie she was a pioneering scientist.

   _____

5. The jury was excused after they had given their verdict.

   _____

6. Please give your application forms to Ms. Pinto or to myself.

   _____

7. The parole board has their next meeting tomorrow.

   _____

8. Each man must do his own work.

   _____

9. Carlos met Mr. Millet when he took a tour of the college.

   _____

10. The baby smiles and laughs, and this delights his parents.

    _____

EXERCISE 14-8   Pronoun Agreement, Reference, and Usage

Rewrite the following sentences to eliminate pronoun agreement, reference, and usage problems. One sentence is correct as written.

> **Example:**   The jury is about to announce their verdict.
>
> *The jury is about to announce its verdict.*

1. Bill is an experienced speaker; this makes a good impression.

   _____

2. The movie what he likes best is *Black Orpheus.*

   _____

3. Bob told Ray that he had written an amusing joke.

   _____

4. Everybody wants the best for their family.

   _____

5. The work that she does is quite important.

   _____

6. The Woods told the Joneses that their house had been burgled.

   _____

7. The financial report was prepared by Mr. Chee and myself.

   _____

8. The dean he was the one who recommended that I take calculus.

   _____

9. The committee hopes to finish their work soon.

_____

10. Either Ms. Green or Ms. Palma can lend you their stapler.

_____

EXERCISE 14-9   Pronoun Agreement, Reference, and Usage

Rewrite the following sentences to eliminate pronoun agreement, reference, and usage problems. One sentence is correct as written.

> **Example:**   The package was sent only to yourself.
>
> *The package was sent only to you.* _____

1. Either Fred or Tom can drive you to work in their car.

   _____

2. The jury finally delivered their verdict.

   _____

3. He heard that the factory it is moving to Georgia.

   _____

4. The package was sent to myself and my sister.

   _____

5. Ms. Jackson she is the evening supervisor.

   _____

6. The reporter which wrote the article on bank fraud did an excellent job.

   _____

7. The team finished its season with six wins and only one loss.

   _____

8. Ariana called Dina to say that she had been invited to join the Forensic Society.

   _____

9. She is honest but diplomatic, which makes her popular with her coworkers.

   _____

10. Somebody left their briefcase in the lobby.

   _____

EXERCISE 14-10   Pronoun Agreement, Reference, and Usage

Rewrite the following sentences to eliminate pronoun agreement, reference, and usage problems. One sentence is correct as written.

> **Example:**   The report what he wrote is excellent.
>
> *The report that he wrote is excellent.*

1. The team reviewed a videotape of their last game.

   _____

2. He felt lonely when his children left home to go to college; he had not expected it.

   _____

   _____

3. Dr. Gordon told Dr. Nichols that her experiment was a success.

   _____

4. Mr. Chun built a house for his wife and himself.

   _____

5. Not only Diane but also Holly found their job very interesting.

   _____

6. The people on the corner they witnessed the accident.

   _____

7. Everyone hopes they will be the one to win the lottery.

   _____

8. Any person that wants to major in biology should talk to Dr. Berry.

_____

9. The letter with insufficient postage was returned to herself.

_____

10. The land what adjoins your property is for sale.

_____

EXERCISE 14-11 | Pronouns in Paragraphs

On separate paper, revise these brief paragraphs to eliminate pronoun agreement, reference, and usage problems. The paragraphs contain some sentences that are correct as written.

1. Christmas bazaars are fun because it offers many gifts to buy and foods to eat. A person that goes to a bazaar usually finds Christmas presents for every member of their family. In addition, they can satisfy their craving for interesting foods.

2. A job and a career are not the same things. On one hand, a job is work that someone does to earn their living. On the other hand, it provides interest and satisfaction as well as money.

3. In Venice, the San Marco cathedral it is covered inside and out with mosaics. Mosaics are pictures what are made of small pieces of marble and glass. The San Marco mosaics portray both saints and biblical scenes.

4. The Cranes they decided to "babyproof" their apartment before he was born. They checked all their rooms to make sure it had no unprotected electrical outlets. They also removed all items what were breakable.

5. Women are the majority of the doctors in the Soviet Union. However, they do not hold most of the jobs with good pay and high status. This is because of prejudice and the attitude that a woman should take a lower-paying job because they will take time off for childbirth and child care.

EXERCISE 14-12   Pronouns in Paragraphs

On separate paper, revise these brief paragraphs to eliminate pronoun agreement, reference, and usage problems. The paragraphs contain some sentences that are correct as written.

1. Some studies suggest that children that watch too much television they sometimes become passive. Such children are not used to making decisions or doing things for themselves. This can be a problem when these children start school.

2. Almost everybody likes to make their working area personal. This makes a person feel that they are not like everybody else. Some people they bring knickknacks or decorations to the office. Others have photos of their families.

3. Ms. Walker she is extremely organized and efficient; this is fortunate because she has many responsibilities. Ms. Walker has three children, and her elderly mother also lives with her. Organizing meals and laundry, supervising homework, taking family members to their doctors' appointments, as well as working nine to five at her job, can put a huge strain on herself.

4. Writing a letter of complaint it is not easy. A person may let themselves become angry; this can mean a letter what does not get results. A person should state the facts concerning their complaint and should not let their emotions carry them away.

5. Becoming a good athlete means more than just playing a sport. For example, a professional basketball player he does more than play ball. He does exercises what increase flexibility, they may run sprints to improve their speed, and perhaps he works out with weights to build strength.

EXERCISE 14-13 Writing with Pronouns

Write sentences using the given pronouns.

> **_Example:_** everyone, his or her
>
> _Everyone here wants to express his or her_
>
> _opinion._

1. their

   _____

2. his or her

   _____

3. whose

   _____

4. its

   _____

5. themselves

   _____

6. our

   _____

7. who

   _____

8. your

   _____

9. he or she

_____

10. that

_____

15 Pronoun Case

Personal pronouns are grouped in three cases, the *subjective, objective,* and *possessive,* according to their functions in sentences.

> **We** have lived here for eight years. (*subjective*)
> The package was addressed to **us.** (*objective*)
> The crew built an addition to **our** house. (*possessive*)

15a In Compound Subjects and Compound Objects

These are the pronouns in the **subjective case:** *I, you, he, she, it, we, they, whoever.* Use a subjective case pronoun in a compound subject.

> INCORRECT: **Me** and Jim are both taking physics.
> CORRECT: Jim and **I** are both taking physics.

These are the pronouns in the **objective case:** *me, you, him, her, it, us, them, whom, whomever.* Use an objective case pronoun in a compound object.

> INCORRECT: Copies of the senator's speech were sent to Ms. Baldwin and **I.**
> CORRECT: Copies of the senator's speech were sent to Ms. Baldwin and **me.**

15b In Predicate Nominatives

Pronouns that are part of predicate nominatives should be in the subjective case.

> INCORRECT: The students elected to the council are Linda and **me.**
> CORRECT: The students elected to the council are Linda and **I.**

15c After *than* or *as*

Sentences using the words *than* or *as* often have elliptical, or incomplete, clauses. Use a pronoun in the case it would be in if the sentence contained the missing words.

INCORRECT:	She is stronger than **me.**
CORRECT:	She is stronger than **I** (am).

INCORRECT:	Kevin likes you as much as **she.**
CORRECT:	Kevin likes you as much as (he likes) **her.**

15d In Appositives

A pronoun in a compound appositive should be in the same case as the noun to which the appositive refers.

INCORRECT:	Only two people—Jane and **me**—had the right answer.
CORRECT:	Only two people—Jane and **I**— had the right answer.

INCORRECT:	He told his secret to only two people—Jane and **I.**
CORRECT:	He told his secret to only two people—Jane and **me.**

15e Before Gerunds and Gerund Phrases

A pronoun preceding a gerund or a gerund phrase should be in the possessive case.

INCORRECT:	The editor liked **them** writing.
CORRECT:	The editor liked **their** writing.

INCORRECT:	The players hated **him** criticizing them after every game.
CORRECT:	The players hated **his** criticizing them after every game.

15f Before Participles and Participial Phrases

A pronoun preceding a participle or a participial phrase should be in the objective case.

INCORRECT:	I could see **his** laughing.
CORRECT:	I could see **him** laughing.

INCORRECT:	In the backyard a child watched **their** splitting logs into firewood.
CORRECT:	In the backyard a child watched **them** splitting logs into firewood.

15g *Who, Whoever, Whom, Whomever*

Who and *whoever* are subjective pronouns.

Who is at the door?
Phil Rizzuto, **who** is now a sportscaster, once played for the Yankees.
Whoever wants this notebook may have it.

Whom and *whomever* are objective pronouns.

To **whom** did you speak?
The committee voted for **whomever** the chairperson had selected.
Whom shall I choose?

(See Exercises 15-1 through 15-11.)

EXERCISE 15-1   Pronoun Case

Identify the case of each personal pronoun.

> subjective   objective   possessive
> **Example:**   I can see <u>him</u> walking with <u>his</u> brother.

1. He repaired the broken headlight.

2. Your car is older than hers.

3. Melville wrote some of his books in Massachusetts.

4. A vacation will give us a chance to rest.

5. Her project was finished before mine was.

6. The rock star was surrounded by fans pushing him and tearing at his jacket.

7. Dr. Alvarez put the x-rays on her desk.

8. She put on her glasses and looked at us.

9. I must call my doctor immediately.

10. Max told the children that he had a surprise for them.

EXERCISE 15-2 Pronoun Case

Choose the correct pronoun in each sentence.

> **Example:** (I), Me and my co-workers are pleased with the new office.

1. The supervisor and (*I, me*) would like to talk to both you and (*he, him*).

2. The people I would like you to meet are (*he and she, him and her*).

3. Send a photocopy of the bill to Mrs. Watkins and (*he, him*).

4. The real negotiating will take place between you and (*I, me*).

5. The work was finished because Ms. Rivera and (*I, me*) stayed here until 9 P.M. to get it done.

6. The last people out of the room were you and (*I, me*).

7. All of (*we, us*) are anxious about the final exam.

8. Both (*he, him*) and his sister are dentists.

9. By coincidence (*they, them*) and the Martins have the same wedding anniversary.

10. Mr. and Mrs. Soriano have no pets because both (*he and she, him and her*) are allergic to dog and cat hair.

EXERCISE 15-3 | Pronoun Case

Choose the correct pronoun in each sentence.

> **Example:** He chose three soloists—Dora, Judy and ~~I~~ (me).

1. The winners—Dora, Ann, and (*me, I*)—sat on the stage.

2. The strange noise in the car worries me more than (*he, him*).

3. Daniel worked hard to improve (*him, his*) speech.

4. Did you see (*our, us*) crossing the street?

5. You are happier about the election than (*us, we*).

6. Two passengers—(*he, him*) and Laura—got off the bus in Pittsfield.

7. Loud music irritates me as much as (*her, she*).

8. The videotape shows (*their, them*) laughing and playing.

9. William is a bit shorter than (*her, she*).

10. All the critics praised (*him, his*) singing of the role of Radames in *Aida*.

EXERCISE 15-4 Pronoun Case

Choose the correct pronoun in each sentence.

> ***Example:*** Have you met Mr. Diaz (~~who~~, ~~whom~~) is the supervisor?

1. I am older than (*her, she*).

2. (*She, Her*) running caught the eye of the track coach.

3. Time passed quickly because of (*his, him*) telling jokes and funny stories.

4. Ms. Santos works just as hard as (*they, them*).

5. The coach watched (*their, them*) practicing.

6. A police officer caught (*his, him*) breaking into a store.

7. Copies of the report should be sent to Mr. Bennet and (*me, I*).

8. She plays volleyball better than (*I, me*).

9. The confidential report was sent to only two people—Mr. Agbi and (*she, her*).

10. They have as much experience as (*him, he*).

EXERCISE 15-5   Pronoun Case—*Who* and *Whom*

Choose the correct pronoun in each sentence.

> ***Example:***   Have you met Mr. Diaz (~~who~~, ~~whom~~) is the supervisor?

1. Give the papers to Ms. Chang, (*who, whom*) is in the first office on the left.

2. Mark Twain, (*who, whom*) wrote *Life on the Mississippi,* was once a riverboat pilot.

3. (*Who, Whom*) did you meet at the business conference?

4. Please see (*who, whom*) is at the door.

5. The singer (*who, whom*) he likes best is Whitney Houston.

6. Alex was the person from (*who, whom*) I heard the news of the union settlement.

7. I want to know (*who, whom*) has won the election.

8. The people will choose (*whoever, whomever*) they want as spokesperson.

9. This is Mrs. Pappas, (*who, whom*) the parents have elected head of the PTA.

10. (*Whoever, Whomever*) starts a fight will be ejected from the game.

EXERCISE 15-6   Pronoun Case

Choose the correct pronoun in each sentence.

Example: The computer assignment was given to (she, her).

1. Her promotion pleases me as much as (*she, her*).

2. Audiences have always enjoyed (*him, his*) dancing.

3. Rita, (*who, whom*) is a lab technician, lives in Chicago.

4. Mr. Chin and (*me, I*) are members of the Rotary Club.

5. Did you hear (*my, me*) laughing at her jokes?

6. She has written more short stories than (*he, him*).

7. We watched (*them, their*) skating around the rink.

8. The winners of the raffle were you and (*she, her*).

9. Two members of the crew—Sandy and (*he, him*)— are cocaptains.

10. Mr. Clayton stared at Jerry and (*her, she*).

EXERCISE 15-7   Pronoun Case

Choose the correct pronoun in each sentence.

> ***Example:***   The audience cheered (~~them~~, *their*) dancing.

1. The crowd did not like (*him, his*) singing of the national anthem.

2. (*He and she, Him and her*) both hope to go to law school.

3. All of (*we, us*) could see (*him, his*) laughing.

4. Rosa, (*who, whom*) the basketball team chose as captain, is a fine athlete.

5. Scholarships were awarded to Gina and (*he, him*).

6. The only person left in the room was (*I, me*).

7. The subcommittee—Carl, Sylvia, and (*me, I*)—will meet tomorrow.

8. The little girl shouts just as much as (*him, he*).

9. (*Whoever, Whomever*) called me hung up before I could answer.

10. You are five years older than (*we, us*).

EXERCISE 15-8   Pronoun Errors

Revise each sentence to eliminate pronoun errors.

> he
> ***Example:***   Both ~~him~~ and his parents are on vacation.

1. Anybody whom needs some help should talk to the professor.

2. Dickinson's poetry is especially meaningful to him and I.

3. He hates broccoli more than us.

4. We could distinctly hear his laughing.

5. You are exactly the same age as her.

6. Can you see his running?

7. She showed her poetry to three friends—Tom, Sam, and I.

8. An ankle injury interrupted him training.

9. They saw our cross-country skiing in the park.

10. The pollen affects him as much as I.

EXERCISE 15-9 | Pronoun Errors

Revise each sentence to eliminate pronoun errors.

> **_Example:_** You and ~~him~~ have a lot in common.
>   *he*

1. Her suggestions really improved us planning of the banquet.

2. I found his working in the basement.

3. Me and him have the same kind of bicycle.

4. You are a better athlete than her.

5. The law school has accepted both you and I.

6. She wants to go out with whoever she pleases.

7. Frank and me need to check inventory.

8. The people whom live here have formed a neighborhood association.

9. Did the theater critics praise him acting?

10. Both me and my sister have two children.

Name _____

Score _____

EXERCISE 15-10 | Pronoun Errors

Revise each sentence to eliminate pronoun errors.

> who
> ***Example:*** I don't know ~~whom~~ was elected to the council.

1. Whomever took the address book should bring it back.

2. Me and you have a lot in common.

3. The person who you thought you recognized is my dentist.

4. Jury notices were sent to him and I.

5. The supervisor who I sent this letter to has not replied yet.

6. I really enjoyed him singing at the concert last night.

7. The prize will be won by whomever wants it most.

8. Him and his brother were born in New Mexico.

9. You have earned more college credits than her.

10. The person to who this letter is addressed has moved.

EXERCISE 15-11   Writing with Pronouns

Write sentences using the given pronouns and phrases.

> ***Example:***   faster than I
>
> *Ramon types faster than I do.*

1. she and I

_____

2. older than he

_____

3. Mr. Vargas and me

_____

4. who

_____

5. whom

_____

6. their singing

_____

7. them laughing

_____

8. you and I

_____

9. to him and me

   _____

10. whoever

   _____

16 Adjectives and Adverbs

An **adjective** modifies a noun or a pronoun.

> A **helpful** *conductor* gave them directions.
> *He* was **helpful.**

An **adverb** modifies a verb, an adjective, or another adverb. Many, but not all, adverbs end in *-ly*.

> He *speaks* **clearly.**
> She is **extremely** *strong.*
> This computer runs programs **very** *quickly.*

A few words can be both adjectives and adverbs, including the following:

fast	far
late	loud

Some adjectives end in *-ly* and are therefore sometimes mistaken for adverbs. Here are some examples:

friendly	costly
lonely	manly

16a Misused Adjective Forms

Use an adverb, not an adjective, to modify a verb, an adjective, or an adverb.

INCORRECT: He worked **cautious.**
CORRECT: He worked **cautiously.**

Do not use an adjective ending in *-ly* if an adverb or an adverbial phrase is needed.

INCORRECT: The operator spoke to us **friendly.**
CORRECT: The operator spoke to us **in a friendly way.**
CORRECT: The operator spoke to us **pleasantly.**

16b Misused Adverb Forms

Use an adjective, not an adverb, to modify a direct object.

INCORRECT: Her supervisor considered her work **excellently.**
CORRECT: Her supervisor considered her work **excellent.**

Use an adjective, not an adverb, after a linking verb.

INCORRECT: His *argument* sounded **logically.**
CORRECT: His *argument* sounded **logical.**

INCORRECT: The *food* tastes **deliciously.**
CORRECT: The *food* tastes **delicious.**

Good and *well*

The words *good* and *well* are often confusing. *Good* is always an adjective. *Well* is usually an adverb meaning "in an excellent way." However, *well* can also be an adjective meaning "healthy" or "satisfactory."

Her test *scores* are **good.**
She *does* **well** on tests.

Today the *patient* feels **well.** (*health*)
Today the *patient* feels **good.** (*mood*)

Action and linking verbs

Some verbs can be both action verbs and linking verbs. Use an adverb after an action verb. Use an adjective after a linking verb.

He *tasted* the wine **carefully.** (*action verb, adverb*)
The food *tasted* **bland.** (*linking verb, adjective*)

People *looked* **curiously** through the door. (*action verb, adverb*)
The children *looked* **curious** and **alert.** (*linking verb, adjectives*)

(See Exercises 16-1 and 16-2.)

16c Comparative and Superlative Forms of Adjectives and Adverbs

For the comparative, add *-er* to most one-syllable adjectives and adverbs. For the superlative, add *-est*.

clean   cleaner   cleanest
fast   faster   fastest

Longer adjectives and adverbs do not take suffixes. Instead, form the comparative with the word *more*. Form the superlative with the word *most*. Never use either *more* or *most* with the suffix *-er* or *-est*.

honest   more honest   most honest
honestly   more honestly   most honestly

careful   more careful   most careful
carefully   more carefully   most carefully

Use the comparative to compare two things. Use the superlative to compare three or more things.

Of the two cars, this one is **more efficient.**
Of all the cars, this one is the **most efficient.**

(See Exercises 16-3 and 16-4.)

16d Double Negatives

In modern English, only one negative word is needed to express a negative idea. Double negatives are not acceptable in today's standard English.

INCORRECT: We **don't** have **nothing** to do.
CORRECT: We **don't** have anything to do.
CORRECT: We have **nothing** to do.

(See Exercises 16-5 through 16-9.)

EXERCISE 16-1 Identifying Adjectives and Adverbs

Identify each italicized word as an adjective or an adverb.

> **Example:**
>   adverb
>   He *quickly* ran back to the car.

1. Most of Emily Dickinson's poems are *short*.

2. We *happily* watched a *lovely* sunset.

3. The atmosphere was *very* tense.

4. *Verifiable* statements are *different* from inferences or opinions.

5. She checked her paper *slowly* and *carefully*.

6. He was driving too *fast*.

7. Our meeting is *extremely* important.

8. Small birds shiver *continuously* to generate heat in *cold* weather.

9. For the survey, people were *randomly* chosen.

10. Some plants do not adjust *easily* to changes in temperature.

EXERCISE 16-2 Choosing Adjectives or Adverbs

For each sentence, choose either the adjective or the adverb.

> **Example:** She worked (~~quiet~~, (quietly)) and did a ((good), ~~well~~) job.

1. At first glance, your math solution seems (*correct, correctly*).

2. The aisles must be kept (*clear, clearly*).

3. These vegetables look (*fresh, freshly*).

4. The court reporter typed (*quick, quickly*) as the witness spoke.

5. I felt (*foolish, foolishly*) playing basketball in a raincoat.

6. I consider that remark (*irrelevant, irrelevantly*).

7. Directed by Ms. Evers, the college chorus sang (*lovely, well*).

8. The fourth-grade children work (*good, well*) together.

9. Kelly did a (*good, well*) job of reorganizing the files.

10. He looked (*nervous, nervously*) at his brother.

EXERCISE 16-3 Choosing the Comparative or Superlative Form

Choose the correct form for each sentence.

> **Example:** This is the (~~less~~ ~~least~~) expensive of the two cars.

1. Yesterday was (*colder, coldest*) than the day before.

2. This car is (*more fuel efficient, most fuel efficient*) than that one.

3. Of the three candidates, Ms. Bates is (*more, most*) experienced.

4. The Empire State Building is (*taller, tallest*) than the Chrysler Building.

5. I think *Celestial Navigation* is (*better, the best*) of all the books Anne Tyler has written.

6. Whole wheat flour is (*more nutritious, most nutritious*) than white flour.

7. Sam is (*younger, the youngest*) of their three children.

8. Of all the experiments, this one was done (*more carefully, most carefully*).

9. This scale is (*more accurate, most accurate*) than the other.

10. Today is the (*hotter, hottest*) day so far this summer.

EXERCISE 16-4 Choosing the Comparative or Superlative Form

Choose the correct form for each sentence.

> ***Example:*** Of the two problems, this one is (*easier*, *easiest*) to solve.

1. Len is (*faster, the fastest*) of all the members of the track team.

2. Of all the cars we looked at, I like this one (*better, the best*).

3. This apartment is (*bigger, the biggest*) than the last one you rented.

4. Of these three air conditioners, this one runs (*more efficiently, the most efficiently*).

5. Last night's football game was (*more exciting, most exciting*) than the one last week.

6. The weather service predicts that tomorrow will be the (*colder, coldest*) day of the winter.

7. Chicken usually has (*less, least*) fat than beef.

8. The bus was (*faster, fastest*) than usual this morning.

9. The (*longer, longest*) you wait to see the dentist, the (*more, most*) problems you will have with your teeth.

10. This model is the (*more expensive, most expensive*) computer in the store.

EXERCISE 16-5   Eliminating Double Negatives

Revise each sentence to eliminate double negatives.

> *Example:*   He can't never get to work on time.
>
> *He can never get to work on time.*
>
> *He can't ever get to work on time.*

1. I can't never reach her on the phone.

   _____

2. He does not believe that nothing bad will happen.

   _____

3. We can't hardly hear you.

   _____

4. Dogs aren't never allowed in the park.

   _____

5. The photograph does not seem to reveal nothing.

   _____

6. We hardly never see you.

   _____

7. I don't feel like doing nothing this morning.

   _____

8. She didn't see nobody in the corridor.

   _____

9. You didn't never answer my letter.

   _____

10. The doctor won't be able to tell us nothing until tomorrow.

    _____

EXERCISE 16-6   Choosing Modifiers

Choose the appropriate word or phrase in each sentence.

> **Example:**   The movie was (~~real~~, *really*) exciting.

1. The storm passed (*harmless, harmlessly*) over the ocean.

2. The patient's blood pressure is up, and he does not look (*good, well*).

3. Several dissatisfied customers looked (*furious, furiously*) as they waited on line.

4. He thinks computers are (*more interesting, most interesting*) than movies.

5. The office does not have (*no, any*) more application forms.

6. I consider this computer program too (*expensive, expensively*).

7. A shrouded figure moved (*ghostly, in a ghostly way*) through the deserted mansion.

8. Most parents consider their children (*real, really*) special.

9. This car's brakes work (*better, best*) than the brakes on that car.

10. The decision of the judges is (*final, finally*).

EXERCISE 16-7 Choosing Modifiers

Choose the appropriate word or phrase in each sentence.

> **Example:** The air was (*thick,* ~~*thickly*~~) with fog.

1. This is the (*easier, easiest*) way to get to Hudson Street.

2. You answered the essay question really (*good, well*).

3. The jury found the defendant (*guilty, guiltily*).

4. She looked (*thoughtful, thoughtfully*) as she read the morning paper.

5. The cashier added up the items (*quick, quickly*).

6. The campus was (*quiet, quietly*) during vacation.

7. The student lounge was redecorated; it looks (*good, well*).

8. The reviewer found the ballet (*delightful, delightfully*).

9. There is (*not hardly, hardly*) any time left before Thanksgiving.

10. The captured man left with the police (*peaceful, peacefully*).

EXERCISE 16-8   Correcting Modifier Errors

Revise the following sentences to eliminate adjective and adverb errors. One sentence needs no revision.

> **Example:**   He didn't have nothing to say.
>
> *He didn't have anything to say.*

1. Most of us feel apprehensively before taking a driving test.

   _____

2. You don't never come to see me no more.

   _____

3. She was the youngest person ever to graduate from Taft High School.

   _____

4. A correct diet helps children to grow strongly.

   _____

5. She did very good on the Civil Service exam.

   _____

6. He looked frightful tired.

   _____

7. Judges at the cooking contest found his cake deliciously.

   _____

8. Rachel is the youngest of his two children.

   _____

9. Be sure to proofread your essay careful.

   _____

10. The guide spoke friendly to groups of tourists at the Statue of Liberty.

    _____

EXERCISE 16-9   Correcting Modifier Errors

Revise the following sentences to eliminate adjective and adverb errors. One sentence is correct as written.

> **Example:**   He looked calm at the crowd.
>
> *He looked calmly at the crowd.*

1. Alice looked curious at the view through the keyhole.

_____

2. People sometimes feel nervously when their boss asks to see them.

_____

3. He is the most strongest of all the weight lifters.

_____

4. The superintendent tries to keep the lobby neatly.

_____

5. I am more tireder than I have ever been before.

_____

6. The poet Keats and the composer Mozart both died young.

_____

7. You and I don't rarely see each other.

_____

8. Two gracefully dancers crossed the stage.

_____

9. Some people consider teaching easily, but it is hard work.

   _____

10. The college debating team did very good yesterday.

    _____

EXERCISE 16-10   Writing with Modifiers

On separate paper, write a sentence using each modifier or phrase.

> **Example:**   well
>
> *Do you prefer steak rare or well done?*

1. intensely

2. friendly

3. logical

4. the most expressive

5. persuasively

6. can do nothing

7. more articulate

8. good

9. spoke quickly

10. ridiculous

EXERCISE 16-11 | Writing with Modifiers

On separate paper, write a sentence using each suggested modifier or phrase.

> **Example:** previously
>
> *Scientists had previously believed that language skills were located in only one part of the brain.*

1. hardly ever

2. gruffly

3. more clearly

4. cleverly

5. lonely

6. the most wasteful

7. ordinarily

8. good results

9. looked happy

10. sensibly

17 Comparisons

When making comparisons, be sure to include everything necessary to make your meaning clear.

17a False Comparisons

Do not compare things that are not essentially similar.

INCORRECT: Your car gets better mileage than Robert.
CORRECT: Your car gets better mileage than Robert's (car does).

17b Incomplete Comparisons

A comparison cannot be made unless at least two things are mentioned.

INCORRECT: Cities are much noisier.
CORRECT: Cities are much noisier than rural areas.

17c Ambiguous Comparisons

Do not make a comparison that has two possible meanings.

INCORRECT: She likes Joe more than Sally.
CORRECT: She likes Joe more than she likes Sally.
CORRECT: She likes Joe more than Sally does.

17d Omitted Comparative Words

Do not omit *than* or *as* in a comparison.

INCORRECT: He is **as** tall, if not taller than, I am.

CORRECT: He is **as** tall **as,** if not taller than, I am.

Use *other* or *else* when comparing one thing with other members of its group.

INCORRECT: She has more credits than any of the students.

CORRECT: She has more credits than any of the **other** students.

(See Exercises 17-1 and 17-2.)

EXERCISE 17-1   Correct Comparisons

Rewrite the following sentences to improve the comparisons. One sentence is correct as written.

> **Example:** She is faster than any of the sprinters on the team.
>
> *She is faster than any of the other sprinters on the team.*

1. Your car has more room than William.

_____

2. This magazine article is better written.

_____

3. Richard is as talented, if not more talented than, Alex.

_____

4. Liz is more opinionated than any of the students.

_____

5. Nathaniel Hawthorne uses more symbols in his writing.

_____

6. You can remember your vacation more clearly than your mother.

_____

7. Pete makes more free throws than anyone on his team.

_____

8. Henry James wrote more novels than Jane Austen did.

_____

9. This office is as crowded today, if not more crowded than, yesterday.

   _____

10. John appreciates good food more than Leslie.

   _____

EXERCISE 17-2   Correct Comparisons

Rewrite the following sentences to improve the comparisons. One sentence is correct as written.

> **Example:**   He has known you longer than Celia.
>
> *He has known you longer than Celia has.*
>
> *He has known you longer than he has known*
>
> *Celia.*

1. Ms. McCoy has known me longer than you.

   _____

2. Debbie types faster than anyone in the room.

   _____

3. His accent is very similar to my grandfather's.

   _____

4. The toll on the Warren Bridge is higher than the Marshall Bridge.

   _____

5. Automobiles are more expensive than six years ago.

   _____

6. I understand you better than Esther.

   _____

7. Jean writes reports more accurately than anyone in the office.

   _____

8. This detergent makes clothes cleaner and brighter.

   _____

9. Ivan's car runs much better.

   _____

10. He was as strong, if not stronger than, she.

    _____

EXERCISE 17-3   Correct Comparisons

Rewrite the following sentences to improve the comparisons. One sentence is correct as written.

> ***Example:***   I have worked with you longer than Antony.
>
> *I have worked with you longer than Antony has.*
>
> *I have worked with you longer than I have with Antony.*

1. My office has more space than Ricardo.

   _____

2. The hospital on North Street is better.

   _____

3. This physics problem is as difficult, if not more difficult than, the one we did yesterday.

   _____

4. Rose is more diplomatic than any of the other students.

   _____

5. This computer is much harder to use.

   _____

6. The roads here are bumpier than the city.

   _____

7. I was as confused, if not more confused than, you.

   _____

8. The noise from the engine sounds much worse.

   _____

9. The nursing students are in class longer.

   _____

10. To Mr. Beaudoin, recognition is just as important, if not more important than, money.

    _____

    _____

18 Shifts

Avoid unnecessary shifts in *number, person, tense, voice,* and *mood.*

18a In Number

Do not shift between the singular and the plural.

INCORRECT: When **a student** first enters college, **they** may be startled by the workload.

CORRECT: When **students** first enter college, **they** may be startled by the workload.

18b In Person

Do not shift needlessly between first-, second-, and third-person pronouns.

INCORRECT: If **a person** waits until the last minute to do Christmas shopping, **you** will experience crowds and long lines.

CORRECT: If **a person** waits until the last minute to do Christmas shopping, **he or she** will experience crowds and long lines.

18c In Tense

When writing about history and literature, you may use either the present or the past tense, but do not shift between tenses.

INCORRECT: Hawthorne **uses** colors symbolically. The color of clothing, for example, **was** a reflection of the wearer's character.

CORRECT: Hawthorne **uses** colors symbolically. The color of clothing, for example, **is** a reflection of the wearer's character.

18d In Voice

Do not shift needlessly between the active voice and passive voice.

INCORRECT: In the movie *Places in the Heart,* Sally Field **portrayed** a widow, and the role of her blind boarder **was acted** by John Malkovich.

CORRECT: In the movie *Places in the Heart,* Sally Field **portrayed** a widow, and John Malkovich **acted** the role of her blind boarder.

18e In Mood

Do not shift needlessly between the indicative, imperative, and subjunctive moods.

INCORRECT: First, **make** a list of the day's tasks. Then, you **should decide** which ones are the most urgent.

CORRECT: First, **make** a list of the day's tasks. Then, **decide** which ones are the most urgent.

(See Exercises 18-1 and 18-2.)

EXERCISE 18-1 | Eliminating Needless Shifts

Revise each item to eliminate needless shifts in number, person, tense, voice, and mood.

> ***Example:*** A person can save money on food if they plant a vegetable garden.
>
> *People can save money on food if they plant a vegetable garden.*

1. When a person applies for financial aid, you have to include a copy of last year's tax returns.

   _____

   _____

2. If an intruder enters the store, they set off an alarm.

   _____

3. Agatha Christie sets many of her mysteries in country houses, and often her characters were members of large families.

   _____

   _____

4. Ella bathed the children first, and then a story was read to them.

   _____

5. Solve the math problem, and you should show your work.

   _____

6. First, break the eggs into a bowl. Then sugar should be added.

   _____

7. Sometimes if a person wants something done right, you have to do it yourself.

_____

_____

8. Always stretch and you should warm up before exercising.

_____

9. She enjoys jazz, but he preferred classical music.

_____

10. Almost every child likes the show "You Can't Do That on Television." They especially enjoy the green slime skits.

_____

_____

EXERCISE 18-2 Eliminating Awkward Shifts

Revise the following items to eliminate awkward shifts in number, person, tense, voice, and mood.

> **Example:** If a person is sick, you should see a doctor.
>
> *If you are sick, you should see a doctor.*

1. Borders of flowers lined the front walk, and half the backyard was filled with a vegetable garden.

   _____

   _____

2. In *Brave New World,* Huxley describes a future in which people were controlled by drugs.

   _____

   _____

3. A person should watch his weight if you want to avoid health problems.

   _____

   _____

4. If my situation were reversed with yours and I was rich, I would help you.

   _____

   _____

5. A camel's shape is awkward, but they make efficient use of food and water.

   _____

   _____

6. If a person wants to be a doctor, you have to take science courses.

   _____

   _____

7. Children usually love potato chips, but spinach is disliked by them.

   _____

   _____

8. People who want to get a tax refund should be sure he or she fills out the income tax forms carefully.

   _____

   _____

9. If I were the boss and he was applying for a job, I would hire him.

   _____

   _____

10. Abraham Lincoln was reelected president in 1864, and in 1865 he is assassinated.

    _____

    _____

19 Sequence of Tenses

Use verb tenses and verb phrases to show when events happen in relation to each other. Look at these examples:

INCORRECT: He *is wearing* a cast because he **breaks** his arm.
CORRECT: He *is wearing* a cast because he **broke** his arm.

The present tense *is wearing* is used because the person currently has the cast. The past tense **broke** is correct because the action of breaking the arm is finished.

In the following pairs of sentences, notice that each correct version indicates which action happened first.

INCORRECT: The fire *spread* to neighboring buildings before the fire trucks **arrived.**
CORRECT: The fire *had spread* to neighboring buildings before the fire trucks **arrived.**

INCORRECT: You *ought* **to file** your financial aid application by now.
CORRECT: You *ought* **to have filed** your financial aid application by now.

INCORRECT: *Finishing* her speech, the Senator **sat** down.
CORRECT: *Having finished* her speech, the Senator **sat** down.

(See Exercises 19-1 through 19-4.)

EXERCISE 19-1 Improving Tense Sequence

Revise these sentences to eliminate errors in tense sequence. Two sentences are correct as written.

> **Example:**   This work ought to be done last week.
>
> *This work ought to have been done last week.*

1. Ironing the bedspread, she put it back on the bed.

   _____

2. I know Detroit well because I live there ten years.

   _____

3. When the crew filled the potholes, the highway was reopened.

   _____

4. The phone stopped ringing before I got to it.

   _____

5. Reaching for a pencil, I knocked over my coffee cup.

   _____

6. All these applications ought to be mailed last week.

   _____

7. Sports fans ought to purchase season tickets by now.

   _____

8. Doctors recommend exercise because it promotes good circulation.

   _____

9. Today the buses are running on time, but yesterday they are not.

   _____

10. Bringing the groceries home, she asked her son to put them away.

    _____

EXERCISE 19-2 Improving Tense Sequence

Revise these sentences to eliminate errors in tense sequence. Two sentences are correct as written.

> **Example:** Beating the eggs, he poured them into the pan.
>
> *Having beaten the eggs, he poured them into the pan.*

1. History remembers Garner only because he is vice president under Franklin Roosevelt.

    _____

    _____

2. After I raked the leaves, I mowed the lawn.

    _____

    _____

3. You ought to reorganize your notebook.

    _____

4. The roast chicken burned before Kelly remembered it.

    _____

5. He would like to win the lottery, but his ticket was not picked.

    _____

    _____

6. Finishing her phone call, she wrote a memo to her boss.

    _____

7. Locking her desk, she walked to the elevator.

_____

8. No one knows where he is; perhaps he leaves and goes home.

_____

_____

9. By last week they ought to file their income tax returns.

_____

_____

10. They had lived in Chicago for two years before they moved to Atlanta.

_____

_____

EXERCISE 19-3 Improving Tense Sequence

Revise these sentences to eliminate errors in tense sequence. Two sentences are correct as written.

> **Example:** Finishing the report, she went home.
>
> *Having finished her report, she went home.*

1. These books ought to be returned yesterday.

   _____

2. The rain had stopped by the time I awoke.

   _____

3. He worked here for ten years when he was transferred.

   _____

4. Her leg is bandaged because she injures it in a skiing accident.

   _____

   _____

5. This letter should have been answered by now.

   _____

6. Working for ten hours, she was tired at the end of the day.

   _____

7. Registering for his classes, Luis went to the bookstore to buy textbooks.

   _____

   _____

8. This week the clinic is not crowded, but last week it is.

_____

9. The secretary says that Ms. Grace leaves for a conference.

_____

10. The car should be inspected two months ago.

_____

EXERCISE 19-4   Improving Tense Sequence

Revise these sentences to eliminate errors in tense sequence. One sentence is correct as written.

> **Example:**   He ought to answer the letter last week.
>
> *He ought to have answered the letter last*
> *week.*

1. Before I reached the elevator doors, they closed.

_____

2. We are visiting the space museum, which is founded in 1965.

_____

3. He would like to be a pilot, but he had poor eyesight.

_____

4. Telephoning his wife, Mr. Colon shut the store and went home.

_____

5. After several counties are flooded, the governor declared an emergency.

_____

_____

6. Having lost my glasses, I could not read the paper.

_____

7. The water filter should be changed last week.

_____

8. The suspect robbed three banks by the time he was caught.

_____

9. The movie ending, the audience left the theater.

_____

10. The road is closed because there is a rock slide yesterday.

_____

20 Sentence Structure

In clear writing, sentences have consistent structure, subjects and predicates match logically, similar elements are expressed in parallel form, and modifiers are placed correctly.

20a Mixed Structure

Finish a sentence using the same structure with which you began it.

INCORRECT: The babysitter read to the children, but no television.
CORRECT: The babysitter read to the children, but he did not let them watch television.

INCORRECT: People who are homeless, how can we help them?
CORRECT: How can we help people who are homeless?

(See Exercise 20-1.)

20b Faulty Predication

A sentence with faulty predication has a poorly matched subject and predicate. Subjects and predicates must match both grammatically and logically.

INCORRECT: Both flexible and strong are characteristics of champion gymnasts.
CORRECT: Both flexibility and strength are characteristics of champion gymnasts.

INCORRECT: The doctor's opinion of this patient is healthy.
CORRECT: In the doctor's opinion, this patient is healthy.

INCORRECT: The reason registration is delayed is because the computer broke down.
CORRECT: The reason registration is delayed is that the computer broke down.

(See Exercise 20-2.)

20c Faulty Parallelism

Use the same part of speech for elements in a series and for elements joined by conjunctions.

INCORRECT: She is an **intelligent, opinionated,** and **contradiction** person. (*adjective, adjective, noun*)

CORRECT: She is an **intelligent, opinionated,** and **contradictory** person. (*adjective, adjective, adjective*)

INCORRECT: He was not only **a hard worker** but also **responsible.** (*noun phrase, adjective*)

CORRECT: He was not only **hardworking** but also **responsible.** (*adjective, adjective*)

Be careful with the placement of correlatives (*not only. . . but also/both . . . and*). Also, repeat words such as *to, a,* and *the* to clarify meaning.

INCORRECT: He not only wanted a raise but also a promotion.
CORRECT: He wanted not only a raise but also a promotion.

INCORRECT: She learned how to draw and paint portraits.
CORRECT: She learned how to draw and to paint portraits.

(See Exercise 20-3.)

20d Dangling Modifiers

A **dangling modifier** does not modify anything in the sentence. Such a sentence must be rewritten to include the person or thing modified.

INCORRECT: Irritated by the noise of a loud party, a phone call to the police was made.
CORRECT: Irritated by the noise of a loud party, a neighbor phoned the police.

20e Misplaced Modifiers

A **misplaced modifier** makes a sentence confusing or silly. Put every modifier as close as possible to what it modifies.

INCORRECT: He only smokes cigars. (*This means he does not do anything else to cigars, such as eat them or shred them.*)
CORRECT: He smokes only cigars (*This means he does not smoke anything else.*)

INCORRECT: I met a man who was German in the library.
CORRECT: In the library I met a man who was German.
CORRECT: I met a German man in the library.

20f Squinting Modifiers

A **squinting modifier** could refer to two elements in a sentence. Place each modifier so that its meaning is clear.

INCORRECT: The teacher announced today there would be a test.
CORRECT: Today the teacher announced that there would be a test.
CORRECT: The teacher announced there would be a test today.

(See Exercises 20-4 through 20-8.)

EXERCISE 20-1   Eliminating Mixed Structure

Rewrite the following sentences to eliminate mixed structure.

> **Example:** Children with physical handicaps, the school is designed for them.
>
> *The school is designed for children with physical handicaps.*

1. You may look at the animals in the zoo, but no food.

   _____

   _____

2. The jury deliberated for a week, but no verdict.

   _____

   _____

3. Police officers who had served in the army, Professor Brown had done a study of them.

   _____

   _____

4. You express your ideas well in your paper, but no organization.

   _____

   _____

5. People who are content with their lot, Samuel envies them.

   _____

   _____

6. Eating properly when under much stress, how can we do it?

_____

_____

7. People wanting refunds, this is the line.

_____

_____

8. Children who are partially deaf, Ms. Martinez teaches them.

_____

_____

9. He speaks very emotionally, but no facts.

_____

_____

10. Growing up in the city, he wrote a book about that.

_____

_____

EXERCISE 20-2   Eliminating Mixed Structure

Rewrite the following sentences to eliminate mixed structure.

> **Example:** Keeping calm in an emergency, I think it is very impor-
> tant.
>
> *I think it is very important to keep calm in an*
>
> *emergency.*

1. Parents who mistreat their children, Nilda hates them.

   _____

   _____

2. The newspaper is well written, but no photographs.

   _____

   _____

3. The hospital on Maple Avenue, Ms. Ross works there.

   _____

   _____

4. The committee met several times, but no report.

   _____

   _____

5. A job with no opportunity for advancement, she is not interested in it.

   _____

   _____

6. People can swim in this pool, but no diving.

_____

_____

7. People who have diabetes, proper diet is important for them.

_____

_____

8. Drugs that cause strong side effects, doctors should prescribe them cautiously.

_____

_____

9. The apartment building is very pleasant, but no laundry room.

_____

_____

10. Neighbors who play their stereo too loud, Alex is irritated by them.

_____

_____

Name _____

Score _____

EXERCISE 20-3 Eliminating Faulty Predication

Rewrite the following sentences to eliminate faulty predication.

> **Example:**   My opinion of the motor vehicle department is inefficient.
>
> *My opinion is that the motor vehicle department is inefficient.*

1. My view of this opera is grand and inspiring.

   _____

   _____

2. Insincerity is a person who cannot be trusted to give an honest opinion.

   _____

   _____

3. Sensible is just as important as intelligence.

   _____

   _____

4. The reason he dislikes the country is because he is allergic to pollen.

   _____

   _____

5. My feeling about the Christmas season is too commercial and starts too early in the year.

   _____

   _____

6. His opinion of your paper is organized and well researched.

   _____

   _____

7. The reason you got the job is because you had better qualifications than the other applicants.

   _____

   _____

8. Contradictory is a quality of many two-year-old children.

   _____

   _____

9. Persistence is a person who never gives up.

   _____

   _____

10. Her idea of a good movie is action and excitement.

   _____

   _____

EXERCISE 20-4 Eliminating Faulty Predication

Rewrite the following sentences to eliminate faulty predication.

> **Example:** The reason the watch broke is because I overwound it.
>
> *The reason the watch broke is that I overwound it.*

1. The reason he succeeds is because he works hard.

   _____

   _____

2. His opinion of your work is thorough and careful.

   _____

   _____

3. Stubbornness is a person who won't change his or her opinion.

   _____

   _____

4. Mr. Riley's feeling about his job is interesting but exhausting.

   _____

   _____

5. Happy is just as important as money.

   _____

   _____

6. Reliability is a car that hardly ever needs repairs.

_____

_____

7. The reason I am late is because the elevator isn't running.

_____

_____

8. His idea of chess is difficult yet intriguing.

_____

_____

9. Strong is as important to an athlete as speed.

_____

_____

10. Her feeling about the city is too crowded and too busy.

_____

_____

EXERCISE 20-5 Eliminating Faulty Parallelism

Rewrite the following sentences to eliminate faulty parallelism.

> **Example:** He not only wanted a raise but also a promotion.
>
> *He wanted not only a raise but also a pro-*
> *motion.*

1. He quickly learned to cook and wash clothes.

   _____

   _____

2. Ruth was a dancer, a teacher, and also she wrote books.

   _____

   _____

3. All parents believe their children are intelligent, charming, and athletes.

   _____

   _____

4. The long tennis match convinced him that he not only needed strength but also stamina.

   _____

   _____

5. He has worked as a stevedore, a bricklayer, and cooking in a fast-food restaurant.

   _____

   _____

6. He not only requested a transfer but also a new schedule.

_____

_____

7. She is not only a good student but also athletic.

_____

_____

8. Nobody here knows how to paint or build bookcases.

_____

_____

9. Ms. Jones has been a library aide, a cashier, and she babysat.

_____

_____

10. Your written work is direct, informative, and insight.

_____

_____

EXERCISE 20-6 Eliminating Faulty Parallelism

Rewrite the following sentences to eliminate faulty parallelism.

> **Example:** She is not only intelligent but also a diplomat.
>
> *She is not only intelligent but also diplomatic.*

1. Patrick not only made ten field goals but also six foul shots.

   _____

   _____

2. He is a musician, a composer, and he also teaches.

   _____

   _____

3. His expression showed both joy and nervous.

   _____

   _____

4. They want to move and buy a house.

   _____

   _____

5. Dress codes not only should apply to students but also to teachers.

   _____

   _____

6. Persistent and confidence made her a successful salesperson.

_____

_____

7. The children seemed lost, worried, and confusion.

_____

_____

8. She is not only a good speaker but also thinks quickly.

_____

_____

9. Last year he learned how to write and tell time.

_____

_____

10. Her job was difficult but a challenge.

_____

_____

EXERCISE 20-7 | Modifiers

Rewrite the following sentences to eliminate dangling, misplaced, and squinting modifiers.

Example: Excited by the performance, the cheering began.

Excited by the performance, the audience began to cheer.

---

1. Frightened by the thunder, his legs shook and his hands trembled.

   _____

   _____

2. Paul cut down a tree with his neighbor.

   _____

   _____

3. The ballet class was taught by a refugee who was from Russia in the big studio.

   _____

   _____

4. The director said today the performance would be canceled.

   _____

   _____

5. Unsuccessful in his job search, disappointment and despair set in.

   _____

   _____

6. Awakened by the alarm, his hand reached to turn it off.

   _____

   _____

7. Monica swept the kitchen floor with her husband.

   _____

   _____

8. Paul met a woman who was Egyptian at the bus stop.

   _____

   _____

9. The reporter said at five o'clock he would interview the mayor.

   _____

   _____

10. Promoted to supervisor, elation filled her heart.

    _____

    _____

EXERCISE 20-8   Modifiers

Rewrite the following sentences to eliminate dangling, misplaced, and squinting modifiers.

> **Example:** At the age of eight, his mother died.
>
> *When he was eight, his mother died.* _____

1. Virginia asked me before I fed the chickens to fix the generator.

_____

_____

2. She only speaks German.

_____

_____

3. Tackled by five football players, the doctor thought his leg might be broken.

_____

_____

4. At the age of five, her father became a pilot for a major airline.

_____

_____

5. I can't believe that he nearly ate the whole pizza.

_____

_____

6. Carlos decided before he went home to finish writing a memo.

_____

_____

7. That kind of vegetarian only eats grains and fruit.

_____

_____

8. Hurt in a car accident, the x-ray showed that his arm was broken.

_____

_____

9. At the age of six, his mother had a second child.

_____

_____

10. It's hard to believe he almost lost forty pounds.

_____

_____

EXERCISE 20-9 Sentence Structure

Rewrite the following items to eliminate errors in sentence structure. One sentence is correct as written.

> **Example:**   They talked and argued, but no fighting.
>
> *They talked and argued, but they did not fight.*

1. The children played baseball, and they jumped rope, but no rollerskating.

   _____

   _____

2. Demanding but fair make her an interesting person to work for.

   _____

   _____

3. He liked the movie because it was moving and for its historical accuracy.

   _____

   _____

4. The London buses, which have conductors as well as drivers do not sell or take tickets.

   _____

   _____

5. The president announced today he would address Congress.

   _____

   _____

6. The senator announced today she would appear at a voter registration rally.

   _____

   _____

7. The play was not only well directed, but superbly acted.

   _____

   _____

8. Walking down Main Street, the sports arena came into view.

   _____

   _____

9. He almost lost fifteen pounds.

   _____

   _____

10. The reason the phone does not work is because the wire is frayed.

   _____

   _____

EXERCISE 20-10 | Sentence Structure

Rewrite the following items to eliminate errors in sentence structure. One sentence is correct as written.

> **Example:** He only eats chicken, not beef or pork.
>
> *He eats only chicken, not beef or pork.*

1. Her photographs are interesting, disturbing, and show a lot of emotion.

   _____

   _____

2. A commercial that is very funny, people do not always remember the name of the product.

   _____

   _____

3. The day before a race, he only eats pasta.

   _____

4. Don Quixote was both romantic and self-deluded.

   _____

5. Diligent and intense are the qualities that make her a good investigator.

   _____

   _____

6. Mrs. Williams asked me before the meeting started to bring her the case files.

   _____

   _____

7. Every day she had to cook and feed the cows.

   _____

8. He ate lunch, read the newspaper, and then a movie.

   _____

   _____

9. Painted by Leonardo da Vinci, people have admired Mona Lisa's smile for centuries.

   _____

   _____

10. Ignorance is someone who does not know all the facts.

   _____

   _____

EXERCISE 20-11 Sentence Structure

Rewrite the following items to eliminate errors in sentence structure. One sentence is correct as written.

Example: Applauding wildly, the game ended.

As fans applauded wildly, the game ended.

---

1. Honesty and kindness are why I like her.

   _____

   _____

2. Encouraged by her friends, Yvette joined the track team.

   _____

   _____

3. My opinion of the book is slow paced, but well researched.

   _____

   _____

4. Aching with pain, the dentist pulled his tooth.

   _____

   _____

5. She can ride a horse, milk a cow, but no bike riding.

   _____

   _____

6. The tenor sang a song about his gloomy future with the soprano.

_____

_____

7. This article is not only misleading but also it has inaccuracies.

_____

_____

8. She is bright, persistent, and enthusiasm.

_____

_____

9. "The Monster," which is a short story about a badly deformed man, I was shocked by it.

_____

_____

10. Alice Walker, who wrote a novel about a young girl had to give up her two children.

_____

_____

PART IV

STYLE AND DICTION

21 Appropriate Word Choice

Formal English, strictly following the conventions of standard English, is appropriate for writing done in college or in a profession, such as term papers and business reports. Informal English, which may include contractions, colloquialisms, and slang, is appropriate for informal writing, such as journals and creative writing.

> INFORMAL: Ms. Jones, the borough president, **blasted** the mayor for vetoing the education bill.
>
> FORMAL: Ms. Jones, the borough president, **strongly criticized** the mayor for vetoing the education bill.

21a Slang

Slang, which is extremely informal, is usually figurative and exaggerated. Most slang terms eventually lose popularity, although some in time are accepted as part of formal language. Slang is inappropriate in college writing.

> SLANG: Some parents **freak out over** their children's wild clothing and hairstyles.
>
> FORMAL: Some parents **are shocked by** their children's wild clothing and hairstyles.

21b Colloquialisms

Colloquialisms are words and expressions used in the everyday language of educated people. Colloquialisms are inappropriate for formal writing.

> COLLOQUIAL: The marathon runner was **pretty** tired at the end of the race.
>
> FORMAL: The marathon runner was **extremely** tired at the end of the race.

21c Jargon

Jargon, or "shop talk," is the special language of people in a particular group or profession. It is usually too technical to be appropriate for most general college writing. Any technical terms you use should always be defined in your writing.

In the example below, most of the terms would not be understood by most members of a general audience. Define any terms your audience may not know.

> Among the equipment on board the satellite will be a cryogenic limb array etalon spectrometer and an active cavity radiometer irradience monitor.

21d Gobbledygook

Gobbledygook is stuffy, pretentious language, often filled with jargon. Use plain language and avoid gobbledygook, which always sounds pompous rather than impressive.

> GOBBLEDYGOOK: The above-mentioned subject invariably sang while he performed his matinal ablutions.
>
> CLEAR: The man usually sang when he washed in the morning.

(See Exercises 21-1 through 21-3.)

EXERCISE 21-1 Avoiding Slang, Colloquialism, and Jargon

Rephrase each of the following sentences in formal, unpretentious English.

1. She always utilizes fresh oregano in her spaghetti sauce.

   _____

2. I paid through the nose for these football tickets.

   _____

3. The defendant's mouthpiece asked for a conference with the judge.

   _____

4. The biology exam was a piece of cake.

   _____

5. She has gone out for her matinal run.

   _____

6. They were pretty impressed by the ambassador's speech.

   _____

7. He wanted to audition for the play, but he chickened out.

   _____

8. I twisted Ed's arm, and he agreed to help you.

   _____

9. Something pretty fishy is going on in the business office.

   _____

10. Fixing the flat tire was a breeze.

    _____

EXERCISE 21-2   Avoiding Slang, Colloquialism, and Jargon

Rephrase each of the following sentences in formal, unpretentious English.

1. Did you touch base with Mr. Roldan?

   _____

2. He crammed all night for the psychology exam.

   _____

3. The two executives plan to interface tomorrow.

   _____

4. The store was packed to the rafters with holiday shoppers.

   _____

5. That guy is a hunk!

   _____

6. The governor hit the roof when he heard the news.

   _____

7. Don't put down his decision until you understand his reasons.

   _____

8. They brown bag it every day to save money.

   _____

9. You can find the math solution if you use your noodle.

   _____

10. He has consented to accept an employment opportunity in Rochester.

   _____

EXERCISE 21-3 Avoiding Slang, Colloquialism, and Jargon

Rephrase each of the following sentences in formal, unpretentious English.

1. The budget crisis is awfully serious.

   _____

2. He had unwisely not made a will before he kicked the bucket.

   _____

3. A guard eyeballed the people entering the bank.

   _____

4. He should not be given the assignment because he is too flaky.

   _____

5. That job opportunity did not pan out.

   _____

6. He nuked a TV dinner in the microwave oven.

   _____

7. She was really ticked off by his lateness.

   _____

8. Your excuse for forgetting the appointment is pretty lame.

   _____

9. The baby went to sleep after her evening ablutions.

   _____

10. She was swamped with extra work all month.

    _____

22 Sexist Language

Language is sexist when it inappropriately designates sex. The words *chairman* and *businessman* are sexist because they imply that only men carry on the activities designated by such titles. In your writing, try to use words that are gender-neutral, substituting, for example, the word *workers* for *manpower,* or *police officer* for *policeman.*

Indefinite singular pronouns such as *everybody* and *someone* can lead to inadvertent sexist language. The word *everybody* is gender-neutral, but because it is singular, pronouns referring to it must also be singular. Look at the following sentence:

Everybody wants the best for *his* children.

Although the sentence above is grammatically correct, the language is sexist because clearly not all parents are men. You can avoid sexist language two ways. First, you can use *he or she* (or *she or he*) when referring to an indefinite singular pronoun. Second, you can use plural words instead of indefinite singular pronouns. Look at the next two examples:

Everybody wants the best for *his or her* children.
All people want the best for *their* children.

Both of the sentences above are correct; you might, however, find it easier to use plural words whenever appropriate. (See Exercise 22-1.)

EXERCISE 22-1 Eliminating Sexist Language

Rewrite each sentence to eliminate sexist language. One sentence is acceptable as written.

> **Example:** The committee will elect a chairman.
>
> *The committee will elect a chairperson.*

1. This office administers the policemen's pension fund.

   _____

2. The mailman arrived earlier than usual today.

   _____

3. Nobody likes losing his job.

   _____

4. Somebody left his briefcase in the lobby.

   _____

5. I estimate that the project will take 100 man-hours.

   _____

6. Each member of the jury was in his or her seat.

   _____

7. Everybody in the crowd was clapping his hands.

   _____

8. The singer is giving a one-man show tomorrow night.

   _____

9. The smallpox vaccine was a boon for all mankind.

_____

10. When the banks were ordered to close, no one could withdraw his money.

_____

23 Exact Word Choice

23a Specific and General Words

Specific words are precise and focused, referring to one subdivision of a general group. **General words** are not focused; they refer to large groups.

GENERAL:	athlete	employee	to work
SPECIFIC:	Patrick Ewing	stenographer	to dig

General words are useful to introduce topics; you should, however, use specific words in your writing for the sake of exactness and precision. Avoid words such as *good, nice, bad, very, great, fine, awfully, well done,* and *interesting,* which are so general that they are nearly meaningless. (See Exercises 23-1 and 23-2.)

23b Concrete and Abstract Words

Concrete words name things that can be seen, touched, heard, smelled, or tasted. **Abstract words** name concepts, ideas, beliefs, and qualities.

ABSTRACT: She discussed the plight of the homeless.

CONCRETE: She described a middle-aged woman wrapped in plastic bags begging on the subway, a mother with two small children huddled over a sidewalk grate, and an elderly man found frozen to death in an alley behind a department store.

When you use abstract words, try to give concrete examples that illustrate and clarify the abstractions. (See Exercises 23-3 through 23-5.)

23c Denotation and Connotation

The **denotation** of a word is its basic dictionary definition. **Connotations** are the associations and emotions that a word suggests. Two words with the same dictionary definition may have quite different connotations.

Overweight is affecting his health.
Obesity is affecting his health.

In your writing, use words with appropriate connotations. Avoid *loaded* words, words with such strong connotations that they can make your writing appear biased. (See Exercises 23-6 and 23-7.)

23d Wordiness and Repetition

Avoid empty words and unnecessary repetition. Write as concisely as possible by eliminating wordy expressions, deleting superfluous words, and reducing larger elements to smaller elements.

WORDY	CONCISE
at this point in time	now
due to the fact that	because
in spite of the fact that	although
in the month of April in the year 1945	in April 1945
the novel that is titled *Celestial Navigation*	the novel *Celestial Navigation*

Concise sentences are stronger and more effective than wordy sentences.

WORDY: The dog that my neighbor owns is a dachshund that has long hair.
CONCISE: My neighbor owns a long-haired dachshund.

(See Exercise 23-8.)

Active and passive voice

Using the *active voice* instead of the *passive voice* often makes a sentence more concise. Look at these two sentences:

WORDY (PASSIVE VOICE):   A gourmet meal that is Chinese **is being cooked** tonight by Claire.

CONCISE (ACTIVE VOICE):   Tonight Claire **is cooking** a gourmet Chinese meal.

Sometimes the passive voice is the most concise way to express an idea:

The governor **was reelected** last year.

(See Exercise 23-9.)

Avoid *it is, it was, there is,* and *there was*

Avoid when possible the constructions *it is, it was, there is,* and *there was.* Although sometimes useful, these constructions often create wordy sentences.

WORDY: It is a fact that smallpox no longer afflicts the world.
CONCISE: Smallpox no longer afflicts the world.

(See Exercise 23-10.)

Redundant elements and repetition

Avoid redundant elements, words that unnecessarily repeat the idea expressed by the word to which they are attached.

REDUNDANT	CONCISE
positive advantages	advantages
advance forward	advance
in the future ahead	in the future
and etc.	etc.
true facts	facts
short in length	short

Repetition, used sparingly, can emphasize a point or complete a parallel structure. Needless or excessive repetition weakens writing. Delete the repeated words or substitute synonyms or pronouns for them.

REPETITIOUS: If parents work and must leave their children with a babysitter, they should interview many babysitters until they find a babysitter who meets their requirements.
CONCISE: Working parents should interview many babysitters until they find one who meets their requirements.

(See Exercise 23-11.)

23e Flowery Language

Like gobbledygook, flowery, pretentious language detracts from writing. Whenever possible, use simple, direct words and phrases.

FLOWERY: The good citizens of the upstanding town of Oneonta were favored by a visit from Senator Valdez, a person of great renown.
DIRECT: The well-known Senator Valdez visited Oneonta last week.

23f Figurative Language

Figurative language, or a figure of speech, uses words in an imaginative (not literal) way to create a strong impression. Three kinds of figures of speech are *simile, metaphor,* and *personification*.

Simile

A **simile** uses the word *like* or *as* to make a comparison between two essentially unlike things.

The snow lay **like** a thick blanket on the fields.
The man's face was as red **as** an apple.

Metaphor

A **metaphor** is a comparison between two essentially unlike things that does not use the word *like* or *as*.

Her mind is an encyclopedia of odd but interesting information.

When using a metaphor, be careful. A mixed metaphor is not logically consistent.

MIXED: The actor's career took off like a rocket but then hit a snag.
CONSISTENT: The actor's career took off like a rocket, but then the engine seemed to fail.

Personification

Personification gives human attributes or qualities to inanimate objects or abstract ideas.

The trees groaned in the wind.

(See Exercises 23-12 and 23-13.)

23g Clichés

Clichés are overused expressions that have lost their freshness and impact. Avoid them and aim instead for originality. Make up new expressions of your own, or change a word or two in an old expression to make it fresh. Here are some expressions to avoid:

beyond a shadow of a doubt
worth its weight in gold
pretty as a picture
a man after my own heart
a sight for sore eyes
tried and true

23h Euphemisms

Euphemisms are words that disguise reality. Although it is not wrong to say *passed on* rather than *died*, many euphemisms have become clichés and have sometimes been used to hide the truth. It is best to avoid most euphemisms.

EUPHEMISTIC: He has a cash-flow problem.
REVISED: He is in debt.

(See Exercise 23-14.)

EXERCISE 23-1   Specific versus General Words

Give two or more specific words for each general word listed here.

> **Example:**   craft (n.)   _*quilting, woodcarving*_

1. work (v.)   _____

2. dancer   _____

3. furniture   _____

4. animal   _____

5. eat   _____

6. blemish (n.)   _____

7. happy   _____

8. plain (adj.)   _____

9. pleasant   _____

10. correct (adj.)   _____

EXERCISE 23-2   Specific versus General Words

Give two or more specific words for each general word listed here.

> **Example:**   property   *house, car* _____

1. emotion   _____

2. change (v.)   _____

3. approve   _____

4. fish (n.)   _____

5. influence (v.) _____

6. doctor (n.)   _____

7. clean (v.)   _____

8. clean (adj.)   _____

9. bright   _____

10. sad   _____

EXERCISE 23-3   Concrete Words

Rewrite each sentence that follows to make it more specific and concrete.

1. Ms. Tejeda is a good nurse.

   _____

2. The concert was interesting.

   _____

3. She is a nice person.

   _____

4. We should do something about drunk driving.

   _____

5. Exercise is good for you.

   _____

6. This room is a mess.

   _____

7. Many people do not like politicians.

   _____

8. Our vacation was pleasant.

   _____

9. Some people are afraid of old age.

   _____

10. The store has some good things on sale.

    _____

EXERCISE 23-4 Writing with Concrete Examples

On separate paper, write two or more sentences giving a specific, concrete example for each generality or abstraction.

1. a heroic deed

2. modern music

3. good food

4. ignorance

5. greed

6. misery

7. intelligence

8. a frightening movie

9. professional athletes

10. generous

EXERCISE 23-5   Writing with Concrete Examples

On separate paper, write two or more sentences giving a specific, concrete example for each generality or abstraction.

1. an interesting book

2. poverty

3. a great artist

4. charitable

5. a bad experience

6. painful

7. a difficult job

8. mercy

9. boring

10. justice

EXERCISE 23-6 | Avoiding Negative Connotations

Rewrite the following sentences, replacing the italicized words with ones that have less negative connotations.

> **Example:** The operation may help straighten his *deformed* leg.
>
> *The operation may help straighten his mis-*
> *shapen leg.*

1. A *scrawny* guard walked into the bank.

   _____

2. The mayoral candidate refused to meet or to debate his *enemy*.

   _____

3. Your suggestions for the party are *dumb*.

   _____

4. His last business venture ended in a *fiasco*.

   _____

5. I admire her *stubborn* refusal to give in to peer pressure.

   _____

6. The defendant's face was *vacant* while the jury announced its verdict.

   _____

7. That store sells *fake* jewelry.

   _____

8. The reporter *distorted* my remarks.

   _____

9. A customer *begged* to see the manager.

   _____

10. A *monstrous* apartment building is being constructed on Main Street.

    _____

EXERCISE 23-7   Writing to Emphasize Connotation

Write a sentence for each word that shows you understand its connotation. Use your dictionary.

1. unsuccessful _____

   barren _____

2. ask _____

   demand _____

3. unpaid _____

   delinquent _____

4. skilled _____

   crafty _____

5. accept _____

   resign oneself to _____

6. cheerful _____

   ebullient _____

7. borrower _____

   debtor _____

8. rich _____

   opulent _____

9. decay _____

   rot _____

10. control _____

    manipulate _____

EXERCISE 23-8 | Eliminating Wordiness

Rewrite each of the following sentences to eliminate wordiness.

Example: The office that Ms. Bowman occupies is getting new carpeting, which should arrive next week.

Next week Ms. Bowman's office is being recarpeted.

---

1. Alice, who is my neighbor, has time for volunteer work in spite of the fact that she has a full-time job.

   _____

   _____

2. It was 1987 that was the year that Martina Navratilova, who is a famous tennis star, won both Wimbledon and the U.S. Open.

   _____

   _____

3. He is of the opinion that judges are too lenient with people who commit white-collar crimes.

   _____

   _____

4. In the month of June in the year 1986 he opened a business that was dry cleaning.

   _____

   _____

5. The house that my uncle lives in was burgled during the time that he was at work.

   _____

   _____

6. I could not call you due to the fact that I had a dentist appointment.

   _____

   _____

7. It is a fact that solar panels can decrease use of electricity.

   _____

   _____

8. In the future ahead, you will be glad you took this job.

   _____

   _____

9. Her report was short in length, but very informative.

   _____

   _____

10. The movie that is called *Alice* was playing all over the city.

   _____

   _____

EXERCISE 23-9 | Using the Active Voice

Rewrite each sentence, changing the passive voice to the active voice. One sentence should not be rewritten.

> **Example:** A new pollution law is being debated by the senators.
>
> *The senators are debating a new pollution*
> *law.*

1. Questions about politics are answered by the state senator in a weekly radio show.

   _____

   _____

2. The color yellow was chosen for his office by Mr. Peters because it is considered by him to look cheerful.

   _____

   _____

3. The novel *Jude the Obscure* is being discussed by us.

   _____

   _____

4. She was promoted to supervisor last month.

   _____

   _____

5. Neighborhood safety measures will be discussed by Officer Anderson.

   _____

   _____

6. The concert was attended by us last night.

   _____

   _____

7. The budget was discussed by the finance committee.

   _____

   _____

8. The broken headlight was replaced by Ms. Jones.

   _____

   _____

9. Tomorrow you will be given a key to the office by Mr. Rios.

   _____

   _____

10. The movie *Psycho* was watched by us.

    _____

    _____

EXERCISE 23-10 Writing Concisely

Rewrite each sentence to make it more concise.

> **Example:** It is well known that children of immigrants grow taller than their parents.
>
> *Children of immigrants grow taller than their parents.*

1. There is a need for parents to learn about infant and child development.

   _____

   _____

2. It is important for people to know how computers will shape the future.

   _____

   _____

3. It was astonishing to Jean when she won a scholarship.

   _____

   _____

4. There was a problem with people being awakened by a car alarm.

   _____

   _____

5. It is a known fact that the future health of babies is affected by prenatal nutrition.

   _____

   _____

6. It is important for people to know the candidates in local and state elections.

_____

_____

7. There is a course on nutrition that is being offered at the Community Center.

_____

_____

8. It was amazing to Dave when he was promoted.

_____

_____

9. There was a strange noise in the engine that worried them.

_____

_____

10. There were customers waiting to enter the store.

_____

_____

EXERCISE 23-11   Eliminating Redundancy

Rewrite each sentence to eliminate redundancies and needless repetition.

> **Example:** He killed himself by committing suicide.
>
> *He committed suicide.*

1. Your plan has several negative disadvantages.

   _____

2. The course syllabus lists all the mandatory requirements.

   _____

3. The seminar is discussing the novels of Henry James and the novels of Edith Wharton.

   _____

   _____

4. Navaho rugs are valuable for the design of the rugs and the workmanship of the rugs.

   _____

   _____

5. The millionaire left all his money to a home for orphans without parents.

   _____

6. After therapy, the improvement in his posture was visible to the eye.

   _____

7. The army retreated backward to the river.

   _____

8. Faulty use of the equipment could cause a fatal death.

_____

9. A salesperson must be civil to customers even when customers are making unreasonable demands.

_____

_____

10. He wanted a promotion for a long time, but, after he got the promotion, the promotion did not make him happy.

_____

_____

EXERCISE 23-12   Writing Using Figurative Language

Use figurative language to complete each item in a vivid and consistent way.

1. The child's eyes _____

   _____

2. The window looked _____

   _____

3. The hands on the clock moved as _____

   _____

4. The prisoner was _____

   _____

5. The dark street looked like _____

   _____

6. The rain seemed like _____

   _____

7. An old Christmas tree _____

   _____

8. The new dishwasher was _____

   _____

9. The people in the emergency room looked like _____

   _____

10. A dog was _____

   _____

EXERCISE 23-13   Writing Using Figurative Language

Use figurative language to complete each item in a vivid and consistent way.

1. At night the bridge looked like _____

    _____

2   Her voice was as _____

    _____

3. The frying bacon _____

    _____

4. The line at the bank moved _____

    _____

5. Her hands were _____

    _____

6. The rain _____

    _____

7. After the interview, she felt _____

    _____

8. His smile was _____

    _____

9. His cough sounded like _____

    _____

10. Her encouraging words were _____

    _____

EXERCISE 23-14 Eliminating Clichés and Euphemisms

Rewrite each sentence to eliminate clichés and euphemisms.

> **Example:** He is a diamond in the rough.
>
> *He is a good person, although his manners are not refined.*

1. He was green with envy when his brother won the lottery.

   _____

2. I don't want you to prevaricate.

   _____

3. The hostages' lives were terminated.

   _____

4. I passed the test by the skin of my teeth.

   _____

5. The defendant was sentenced to five years in the state correctional facility.

   _____

6. In a large family there is never a dull moment.

   _____

7. Breaking a bad habit is easier said than done.

   _____

8. The senator believes that the government should not disseminate disinformation.

   _____

9. Only a few weeks after his heart attack, he felt as strong as an ox.

   _____

10. The rain had stopped in the blink of an eye.

    _____

24 Correct Word Choice

If you are confused about word choice, consult your dictionary. Doing so will help you avoid **malapropisms,** inappropriate and unintentionally funny uses of words (e.g., saying "historical fit" instead of "hysterical fit"). The dictionary will also help you choose between **homonyms,** words that sound alike but that have different meanings and spellings. (See Exercises 24-1 through 24-6.)

EXERCISE 24-1   Correct Word Choice

Choose the correct word in each of the following sentences.

> ***Example:***   Everyone (~~accepts~~, (expects)) her to win the election.

1. Did you (*lose, loose*) your wallet?

2. After the (*wreak, wreck*), trucks towed the cars away.

3. Will higher gas prices (*altar, alter*) our driving habits?

4. She made an (*allusion, illusion*) to *King Lear*.

5. Does the (*presence, presents*) of so many observers make you nervous?

6. She is a (*principle, principal*) dancer at the ballet.

7. He has resigned from the town (*council, counsel*).

8. The patient is not (*conscience, conscious*) yet.

9. She is stronger (*than, then*) she looks.

10. Money is at the (*root, route*) of their problems.

EXERCISE 24-2   Correct Word Choice

Choose the correct word in each of the following sentences.

> ***Example:*** He is nervous about speaking in the (~~presents~~, presence) of so many famous people.

1. She (*past, passed*) the chemistry test.

2. (*There, Their, They're*) is a smoke detector in the hall.

3. Is this business (*fiscally, physically*) sound?

4. I (*though, thought*) the concert started at 7 P.M.

5. We cannot afford to (*waist, waste*) our natural resources.

6. This block is the (*cite, site*) of our proposed factory.

7. She has decided to (*accept, except*) that job offer.

8. No one should be allowed to (*flaunt, flout*) the law.

9. Their religious (*beliefs, believes*) prohibit smoking and drinking.

10. The person (*who's, whose*) name is drawn will win the door prize.

| **EXERCISE 24-3** | **Correct Word Choice** |

Choose the correct word in each of the following sentences.

> **Example:** They are expanding (~~there~~, *their*) business.

1. She won the most (*resent, recent*) primary election.

2. No one knew (*where, were*) the treasures of Troy had been hidden.

3. He decided to (*complain, complaint*) to the manager.

4. The children are happy because (*there, their, they're*) going to the beach.

5. He could not decide (*weather, whether*) to retire or to keep working.

6. You will find him rather stubborn and (*independence, independent*).

7. There have been two major storms in the (*past, passed*) week.

8. We will get (*though, through*) this work by five o'clock.

9. The dog growled at the (*sight, site*) or sound of an intruder.

10. Would you (*advice, advise*) me to sell my stocks?

EXERCISE 24-4   Correct Word Choice

Choose the correct word in each of the following sentences.

> ***Example:***   She is a very (~~independence~~, (independent)) person.

1. It is (*to, too, two*) cold (*to, too, two*) go jogging.

2. Read the (*hole, whole*) article before judging it.

3. A long, frustrating day had tried his (*patients, patience*).

4. A convertible sofa has a (*dual, duel*) purpose.

5. Turn back to the (*preceding, proceeding*) page.

6. There are (*know, no*) more copies of that magazine left.

7. The curriculum is (*being, been*) revised.

8. Mr. and Mrs. Murphy are visiting (*there, their, they're*) son.

9. One should not give in to (*pier, peer*) pressure.

10. The medicine (*prescribed, proscribed*) by Dr. Castle contains no caffeine.

EXERCISE 24-5 Writing with the Correct Words

On separate paper, write a sentence for each of the given words.

> **Example:** fourth
>
> *She is the fourth candidate to speak.*

1. extinguish

2. distinguish

3. they're

4. their

5. close

6. clothes

7. quiet

8. quite

9. personal

10. personnel

EXERCISE 24-6 Writing with the Correct Words

On separate paper, write a sentence for each of the given words.

> **Example:** advice
>
> *Your advice helped me choose the right computer.*

1. expect

2. except

3. physical

4. fiscal

5. complain

6. complaint

7. site

8. sight

9. allot

10. a lot

PART V

PUNCTUATION AND MECHANICS

25 End Punctuation

The three **end punctuation marks** are the *period,* the *question mark,* and the *exclamation point.*

25a The Period

Use a **period** at the end of a sentence that:

1. Makes a statement.
2. Makes a request.
3. Expresses a mild command.
4. Gives directions.
5. Asks an indirect question.
6. Makes a request politely expressed as a question.

Ms. Colon is head of the Parents Association.
Please give to the United Way.
Write your name on the top line.
Go to the end of the hall and turn right.
She wonders whether aspirin has side effects.
Will you please mail this package.

Use a period after most abbreviations and initials, but not after abbreviations of metric measurements, acronyms, or abbreviations of businesses and agencies.

Mr. Reed E. Smith has enlisted in the U.S. Army.
The syringe is filled with 4cc of medication.
He joined ASCAP last year.

(See Exercise 25-1.)

25b The Question Mark

Use a **question mark:**

1. At the end of a sentence that asks a direct question.
2. At the end of an interrogative element in another sentence.
3. In parentheses, to express doubt about a date or a word.

Has the exam schedule been posted**?**
Are my children safe**?** he wondered.
Alaric (A.D. 370**?**–410) was a Visigoth king who conquered Rome.

In formal writing, use a capital (*uppercase*) letter to begin a question that follows an introductory element. Less formal writing allows a lowercase letter.

FORMAL: The essay asks, **C**an we afford to continue polluting the atmosphere**?**
INFORMAL: He asked, **d**id I lock the front door**?**

(See Exercise 25-2.)

25c The Exclamation Point

Use an **exclamation point** at the end of a sentence, word, or phrase to express surprise, emotion, or emphasis. Do not overuse the exclamation point. It is rarely found in formal writing.

Ridiculous**!**
You will never beat us**!**
What a mess**!**

(See Exercises 25-3 through 25-6.)

EXERCISE 25-1 Periods

Put periods where necessary.

> **Example:** Mrs. Jackson is a state senator.

1. They were married on Dec 15 in Lenox, Massachusetts

2. Support your local Red Cross

3. The NAACP has chapters all over the U S

4. Dr Levin ordered 2cc of medication

5. Will you kindly move your car

6. Go to Dr Hall's office and give her this form

7. Mrs Matias asked if the package has arrived

8. File your income tax returns early

9. Please make a donation to the scholarship fund

10. Movies are very often based on books

EXERCISE 25-2   Question Marks

Put question marks where necessary. One sentence is correct as written.

> **Example:**   Where is the cafeteria?

1. Have you seen Mrs. Santa Rita.

2. Aesop (620 –560 B.C.) wrote fables.

3. Will you please be quiet in the halls.

4. The historian wonders, Have we learned from our past errors.

5. The letter said I had won the lottery—could I be dreaming—and would receive the first check in five days.

6. Ben Jonson (1572 –1637) wrote both prose and poetry.

7. Is the transit system running this morning.

8. Did I feed the cat he wondered.

9. Scientists often ask, Are we ruining our environment.

10. Is it wise to change jobs so often.

EXERCISE 25-3 End Punctuation

Put periods, question marks, and exclamation points where necessary.

> **Example:** Does the library close at nine?

1. Put the package on the table

2. The war in the Persian Gulf stirred up strong feelings

3. Our supervisor asked if we could work overtime

4. What is best for my child asks every working parent

5. Please fill out the application form carefully

6. E M Forster wrote "My Wood," a famous essay

7. Will you please file these papers

8. When was *The Scarlet Letter* first published

9. Ramona wondered, should I ask for a raise

10. Sir Thomas Malory (–1471) is one of many authors to write about Arthurian legends

| **EXERCISE 25-4** | **End Punctuation** |

Put periods, question marks, and exclamation points where necessary.

> ***Example:***   The seminar will cover the causes of the Civil War.

1. The most relevant question is, How can education be improved

2. Will you please help me move this desk

3. Water the roots well after transplanting bushes and shrubs

4. Did new medicine or better sanitation reduce tuberculosis

5. Thomas Hardy's novel *Jude the Obscure* was published serially in 1894

6. How can the plight of the homeless be alleviated

7. Does the candidate understand the issues the reporter asked

8. Get out

9. The survey taker asked shoppers what they were buying

10. Mr and Mrs Sawyer own a stationery store

EXERCISE 25-5 | End Punctuation

Put periods, question marks, and exclamation points where necessary.

Example: She asked if there was anything she could do to help.

1. The lead editorial questions whether the tax hike is necessary

2. Who will be elected governor on November 4th

3. The weather is certainly mild, isn't it

4. Turn to page 3 and answer all the questions

5. Which newspaper do you think covers the news best

6. Does this medicine have side effects the patient wondered

7. After a long day's work, she is tired

8. She asked the question, Was the Soviet occupation of Afghanistan similar to America's involvement in Vietnam

9. A ridiculous idea

10. Please keep the block clean

EXERCISE 25-6   End Punctuation

Put periods, question marks, and exclamation points where necessary.

> **Example:**   How far is it to Pittsburgh?

1. Was Jigoro Kano the inventor of judo

2. Dr King went to veterinary school in Ithaca, N Y

3. How safe are kerosene heaters she asked the salesperson

4. Many people wondered why the congresswoman did not run for president

5. The commentator wondered, Is it possible to eliminate child abuse

6. The book is really exciting

7. Several customers asked if the sale was still in progress

8. Please help me move this file cabinet

9. Drive three blocks down Oak Drive and then turn right

10. Much Native American poetry consists of songs for particular occasions

EXERCISE 25-7   Writing with End Punctuation

On separate paper, write three or more sentences on each suggested topic. Use appropriate end punctuation.

1. Three questions to ask your mayor

2. Registration this semester

3. Your breakfast this morning

4. Your next-door neighbor

5. The way you speak

6. A relative's hands

7. Your most valuable possession

8. How to speak to a two-year-old child

9. A peculiar experience

10. Your favorite joke

26 The Comma

26a Between Coordinate Elements

Use a comma:

1. Between two independent clauses joined by a coordinating conjunction.
2. To separate three or more items in a series.
3. Between coordinate adjectives.

Athletes in sports like gymnastics tend to be quite young, but professional golfers can play into their 40s and 50s. (*comma between two independent clauses joined by a coordinating conjunction*)

Racine, Montaigne, and La Rochefoucauld are three well-known French writers. (*commas separating three words in a series*)

In the park were children playing on the swings, dog owners walking their pets, and joggers running on the paths. (*commas separating three phrases in a series*)

Duguay stole the hockey puck, he passed it to Dionne, and Dionne scored. (*commas separating three clauses in a series*)

He refused to go into the cold, dark, damp cellar. (*commas between coordinate adjectives*)

Do not use a comma between cumulative adjectives, the order of which cannot be reversed.

He wore an expensive gold watch. (*No comma is needed. The order of* expensive *and* gold *cannot be reversed.*)

(See Exercise 26-1.)

26b After Introductory Words, Phrases, and Clauses

Use a comma:

1. After an introductory word or expression.
2. After an introductory verbal or verbal phrase.
3. After an introductory series of prepositional phrases.
4. After any introductory phrase if misreading might occur without the comma.
5. After an introductory adverb clause.

Yes, the matinee starts at 2 P.M. (*comma after an introductory word*)

Looking thoughtful, he picked up the telephone. (*comma after a verbal phrase*)

In the novel *Pudd'nhead Wilson* by Mark Twain, a nurse exchanges her own child for her master's son. (*comma after an introductory series of prepositions*)

Before brushing, his hair was tangled and unruly. (*comma after an introductory phrase to avoid misreading*)

Although woolen clothing is warmer than that made of acrylic, wool is also more expensive and more difficult to wash. (*comma after an introductory adverb clause*)

(See Exercise 26-1.)

26c Before Certain Terminal Elements

Use a comma:

1. To set off an element contrasting with what precedes it.
2. Before a short interrogative element at the end of a sentence.

Many people work for recognition, not for money. (*comma setting off a contrasting element*)

The Macintosh computer is certainly easy to use, isn't it? (*comma before a short interrogative element*)

Commas and terminal adverb clauses

In general, do not use a comma before a terminal adverb clause.

The vegetable garden was damaged *when rabbits got in under the fence.* (*no comma*)

The preceding rule does have several exceptions. Use a comma before a terminal adverb clause that begins with:

1. *although* or *even though*.
2. *since* or *while* when expressing cause or condition (but not time).
3. *because* if the clause does not modify the nearest verb.
4. *so that* when indicating result (but not purpose).

Registration went smoothly, *even though thousands of students were signing up for classes*. (*comma before* even though)

He should not eat peanut butter, *since he is allergic to it*. (*comma before* since, *indicating cause*)

She has felt fine since she began jogging. (*no comma before* since, *indicating time*)

I knew Tommy was hiding, *because the principal was looking for him*. (*comma before* because, *indicating that the clause modifies the verb* knew)

I knew Tommy was hiding *because the principal was looking for him*. (*no comma before* because, *indicating that the clause modifies the verb* was hiding)

That television show is both entertaining and nonviolent, *so that both parents and children enjoy it*. (*comma before* so that, *indicating result*)

He drives to work early *so that he can avoid the rush hour traffic*. (*no comma before* so that, *indicating purpose*)

(See Exercise 26-2.)

26d Around Interrupting Elements

Use commas to set off:

1. Nonessential appositives and adjective clauses.
2. Internal adverb clauses.
3. Conjunctive adverbs and transitional phrases.
4. Words identifying a quotation's source.
5. Parenthetical expressions.
6. Words in direct address.
7. Elements of dates.
8. Elements of addresses.

Pearl Buck, who was the daughter of American missionaries, grew up in China. (*commas setting off a nonessential adjective clause*)

Two-year-old children, as experienced parents know, are stubborn. (*commas setting off an internal adverb clause*)

Rosalyn Carter, on the other hand, was a very active First Lady. (*commas setting off a transitional phrase*)

"Bailey," wrote Maya Angelou of her brother, "was the greatest person in my world." (*commas setting off the source of a quotation*)

Children, according to an old saying, should be seen and not heard. (*commas setting off a parenthetical expression*)

Is it true, Arthur, that you are moving to Nevada? (*commas setting off a word in direct address*)

She was born on Saturday, August 7, 1971, at 4:48 P.M. (*commas separating elements in a date*)

His office is at 429 Riverside Drive, New York, NY 10025. (*commas separating elements in an address, with no comma between the state and zip code*)

(See Exercise 26-3.)

26e Misused Commas

Do *not* use a comma in the following cases:

1. Between a subject and its predicate.
2. Between a verb and its complement.
3. Between cumulative adjectives.
4. Between the two parts of a compound subject, a compound verb, or a compound complement.
5. Between two dependent clauses joined by *and*.
6. Between the parts of a comparison.
7. Before an opening parenthesis.

(See Exercises 26-4 through 26-10.)

Name _____

Score _____

EXERCISE 26-1　Comma with Series and Introductory Elements

Place commas where necessary in the following sentences.

> **Example:**　The coat is available in red, green, blue, and gray.

1. Bellini Mantegna Veronese and Titian were Italian painters.

2. That dark leather jacket is available in black blue gray and brown but this coat is available only in black and gray.

3. No I did not borrow your electric sander.

4. Loud enthusiastic applause rang through the hall yet the famous actor had not entered.

5. On the top shelf of the hall closet you will find an old pair of gloves.

6. The week before he had two job interviews.

7. The airplane carried tourists visiting Europe for the first time students taking advantage of discount fares and executives involved in international business.

8. Hoping to lower his cholesterol level he changed his diet.

9. Louisa May Alcott wrote plays for her family in the 1840s her first story was published in 1852 and her novels appeared from 1869 to 1886.

10. Because Mr. and Mrs. Pertini live in Switzerland they have learned to speak German and French.

EXERCISE 26-2 Commas with Terminal Elements

Place commas where necessary in the following sentences. Two sentences need no commas.

> **Example:** This is an express bus, isn't it?

1. He forgot to latch the gate so that all the cows got out of the pasture.

2. Beethoven continued to compose music even though he had become deaf.

3. Movie attendance may decline if ticket prices are raised.

4. He does wood carving for pleasure not for money.

5. Some people enjoy high-pressured jobs but others dislike them.

6. Lyn must be careful not to overexert herself since she has asthma.

7. The movie was quite frightening wasn't it?

8. The dancer is very strong although he is short and slim.

9. One bird watched from the fence while another bird ate strawberries.

10. This bus doesn't stop in Billings does it?

EXERCISE 26-3 Commas with Interrupters

Place commas where necessary in the following sentences.

Example: Children, she insists, should learn at their own pace.

---

1. "The mass of men" wrote Henry David Thoreau "lead lives of quiet desperation."

2. Cats contrary to popular belief do not always survive falls.

3. Ms. Lorenzo who was once in the Army is now in college.

4. The senator however does not want a tax increase.

5. I would like ladies and gentlemen to introduce our guest speaker.

6. She was born on Thursday June 26 1975.

7. An understanding of math is needed for example in both physics and chemistry.

8. The congressional hearings as television viewers know preempted the regular programming.

9. They moved to Maple Street Hinsdale Massachusetts 01235.

10. Ann's project a model of the human eye won third prize at the school science fair.

EXERCISE 26-4 | Comma Uses

Place commas where necessary in the following sentences.

> **Example:** When it is winter, the days are short.

1. When the speed limit was lowered fewer accidents occurred.

2. The famous photograph of Anne Frank shows a pretty sensitive face.

3. To understand a country well one must live there for a time.

4. The city's Public Theater does seven plays a year and it also has a children's program.

5. In a long article on the front page of the paper Ms. Fischer analyzed the problems of the homeless.

6. A rural veterinarian treats horses cows pigs sheep and goats.

7. You must not however neglect your responsibilities.

8. Before repainting the walls must be scraped and sanded.

9. Freud who was born in Austria moved to England in 1938.

10. This stain can be removed can't it?

EXERCISE 26-5   Comma Uses

Place commas where necessary in the following sentences. One sentence is correct as written.

> **Example:**   Two police officers, Jackson and Rivera, were on patrol.

1. Marching into the ring were clowns wearing baggy pants jugglers tossing balls into the air and acrobats turning somersaults.

2. Susan is an artist her sister is a psychologist and her brother is a musician.

3. The college has a work-study program doesn't it?

4. Because chicken pox is not usually serious a vaccine for it had not been developed until recently.

5. Grumbling he retyped the letter.

6. Sighing she picked up the scattered papers.

7. All babies as every parent knows are not alike.

8. Stubbs and Munnings two English painters are famous for pictures of horses.

9. He inherited his grandfather's old silver watch.

10. The libraries are not open nor is the post office.

EXERCISE 26-6   Comma Uses

Place commas where necessary in the following sentences.

> ***Example:*** A new traffic light, on the other hand, would reduce accidents.

1. The president however vetoed the civil rights legislation.

2. The economy many experts believe will begin to improve.

3. Bob Cousy was a great basketball player even though he was not particularly tall.

4. Mrs. Jackson who is an x-ray technician graduated from the local community college.

5. This science fiction novel contains much fiction little science.

6. When Jermaine joined the Army he was eighteen years old.

7. Whales look like fish yet they are actually mammals.

8. One child erased the board another collected papers and a third straightened up the bookshelves.

9. In the play *The Glass Menagerie* by Tennessee Williams a mother dominates her shy crippled daughter.

10. Yes fiber is found in fruits vegetables and grains.

EXERCISE 26-7 Comma Uses

Place commas where necessary in the following sentences. One sentence is correct as written.

> **Example:** Ms. Dyson, who has two children, is a lawyer.

1. I ask my fellow citizens for your votes on Election Day.

2. City buses many people think are seldom on schedule.

3. The filter was clogged so water ran slowly from the faucet.

4. Chimpanzee life was not well understood before Jane Goodall began her studies in the African forest.

5. In one morning she weeded the garden mowed the lawn cleaned the children's wading pool and washed the car.

6. This block which was once run down has improved in recent years.

7. Franklin Roosevelt died suddenly of a cerebral hemorrhage on April 12 1945.

8. She speaks German well since she grew up in Munich.

9. Hoping to graduate sooner than scheduled she took extra credits for three semesters.

10. Even though he is eighty years old Mr. Green still has excellent hearing and eyesight.

EXERCISE 26-8 | Comma Uses

Put commas where necessary in the following sentences.

> **Example:** When cornered, animals may fight instead of flee.

1. The camp counselors came from Canada France Great Britain and Italy.

2. This zoo is best suited for reptiles and small mammals not for large animals such as lions and elephants.

3. As soon as the timer rings remove the container from the oven.

4. When cooked rice expands to several times its original volume.

5. The winter as the weather bureau had predicted was unusually mild.

6. The fare raise moreover will hurt the poor in particular.

7. Mr. Villanueva gave a brief informative report.

8. She returned the merchandise to the store in Dayton Ohio on May 12 1987.

9. Ms. Grey a computer programmer knows several computer languages.

10. On the other hand small family size allows parents to give each child more time and attention.

EXERCISE 26-9 Writing with Commas

On separate paper, write sentences using the suggested topics. Place commas where necessary.

> **Example:**   A dead car battery.
>
> *The battery was dead, so the car would not start.*

1. Ms. Lucas a nurse and my neighbor

2. A person who is slim but athletic

3. What happened when it rained

4. Three scholarship winners

5. Chemistry and the math prerequisite

6. An alley that is dark and isolated

7. A dog and fire engines

8. Emphasizing that it has rained all week

9. Landfills and recycling

10. Distinguishing one kind of cereal from another

EXERCISE 26-10 Writing with Commas

On separate paper, write sentences using the suggested topics. Place commas where necessary.

Example: Giving a negative answer to a question

No, this is not the bus to Oakland.

---

1. Why the room was repainted

2. What to do upon seeing Mr. Han

3. A place both unknown yet familiar

4. Mrs. Negron's three children

5. The date of your high school graduation

6. A question to Emma about the location of the cafeteria

7. Two kitchen appliances that are not working

8. Clients at a day-care center

9. Concluding that a schedule change is needed

10. Giving a positive answer to a question

27 The Semicolon

Use a **semicolon:**

1. To link two independent clauses not joined by a coordinating conjunction.
2. To separate two independent clauses joined by a coordinating conjunction if one or both clauses have internal commas or are complex.
3. To separate items in a series if the individual items are long or contain commas.

The desert looks lifeless; its appearance, however, is deceptive.

Penicillin, which was observed in 1928 to have antagonistic effects on bacteria, is a highly effective drug; but its use is limited because, though it causes fewer side effects than many other drugs, many people are allergic to it.

Thomas Jefferson's diverse talents are shown in his many roles: member of the committee that drafted the Declaration of Independence; governor of Virginia from 1779 to 1782; minister to France at the beginning of the French Revolution; and, in 1800, president of the United States.

Do not use a semicolon between noncoordinate elements. (See Exercises 27-1 and 27-2.)

EXERCISE 27-1 | Semicolons

Place semicolons where necessary in the following sentences. One sentence is correct as written.

> ***Example:*** One must not take medicine without thought; one must weigh a medicine's benefits against its side effects.

1. Professional athletes make huge salaries their careers, however, are often quite short.

2. Registration at the college, which used to take a student six or seven hours to complete, now can be completed in approximately two hours a computerized system has reduced the time needed to check for scheduling conflicts and closed class sections.

3. A parent must have the skills of many different people: a nurse, to take care of illness, a diplomat, to settle quarrels, and a teacher, to help with home-work.

4. Ann Lee, an important Shaker leader who was imprisoned for her beliefs, immigrated to America in 1774 with only eight followers, but, by 1826, there were eighteen Shaker communities, all large and prosperous, in eight states.

5. Dyslexia and intelligence are not related; many bright, creative people have reading or learning disabilities.

6. The lack of gravity in space has many effects on astronauts who have been in space for long periods of time: reduced blood volume, the heart not having to work as hard in space as on earth, muscle deterioration, caused by lack of resistance, and calcium loss from the bones.

7. Many officials would like to ban polystyrene foam, a material used as packag-ing by some fast-food restaurants, the material, commonly known by the trade name of Styrofoam, has only a short period of usefulness yet is not biodegrad-able.

8. Alsace, which at various times has belonged to Germany and to France, is now a part of France, French is its official language, although half its inhabi-tants speak Alsatian, a dialect similar to German.

9. Radon is a naturally occurring radioactive gas, it can be dangerous to people if concentrations of it build up in unvented areas such as basements.

10. The prefixes "ante" and "anti" look very similar their meanings, however, are quite different.

EXERCISE 27-2 | Semicolons

Place semicolons where necessary in the following sentences. One sentence is correct as written.

> ***Example:*** Separating garbage for recycling can be irritating; the benefits, however, are worth the trouble.

1. Overpopulation is a problem in many countries some nations have laws governing the number of children a couple may have.

2. One estimate claims that there are 14 million camcorders in the United States many parents use them to record the milestones in their children's lives.

3. In 1945, after its surrender at the end of World War II, the nation of Japan underwent many changes two of the most important changes, which altered the nation considerably, were restrictions on the military and sweeping land reforms.

4. Some chemical compounds have mirror-image pairs, meaning that some molecules are left handed and some are right handed, but despite the similarities the two types of a chemical pair may have very different effects.

5. In recent years, the ranges of the following animals and plants have been shifting northward: the woodland deer mouse, which has big ears and a long tail, the Virginia opossum, which is moving well into New England, and the Calypso bulbosa orchid, which is a heat-sensitive species.

6. George Washington, according to his biographer, James Thomas Flexner, was "the only Virginia founding father to free all his slaves"; all of them were freed in December 1800.

7. Several recent movies were inspired by comic books two examples are *Batman* and *Dick Tracy*.

8. For generations, people have used various products in order to avoid, reduce, or remove wrinkles: for example, creams, moisturizers, and lotions, in the last several years, injections of collagen, most recently, electrical stimulators that apply mild electric current to the skin.

9. Collard greens are thought of as a typically southern American food, they are, however, also very popular in India.

10. There has been a great deal of publicity about America's aging population and the need for nursing homes, surprisingly, researchers found that most elderly people live and eventually die at home, among family.

EXERCISE 27-3   Writing with Semicolons

Using the suggested topics, write sentences that require semicolons. Use separate paper.

> **Example:**   The difference between a job and a career
>
> *A job is what a person works at to earn money; a career, on the other hand, also brings a person satisfaction and fulfillment.*

1. Two kinds of restaurants in your neighborhood

2. A person of many different talents

3. Different meanings of the prefix "in-"

4. Places to study at your college

5. A job you loved

6. A job you hated

7. The first time you met someone who became important to you

8. A place that frightens you

9. Learning a new skill

10. Feeling out of place in a situation

28 The Colon

The **colon** introduces elements that illustrate or expand the preceding part of the sentence. Use a colon:

1. Before elements introduced formally, such as quotations or a series of items.
2. Before formal appositives.
3. Between two independent clauses when the second clause explains the first.

The core curriculum at this university includes the following courses: English, history, math, science, and languages.

Marian Evans is better known by her pen name: George Eliot.

The sleet was dangerous: it had caused ten accidents.

The colon is used in salutations and bibliographical entries.

Dear Dr. Strauss: (*after a salutation in a formal letter*)

New York: Macmillan (*between the city and the publisher in a bibliographical entry*)

Old New York: Yesterday and Today (*between a title and its subtitle*)

Do not use a colon after a form of the verb *to be,* after a preposition, or between a verb and its object. (See Exercise 28-1.)

EXERCISE 28-1   Colons

Put colons where necessary in the following sentences. One sentence is correct as written.

> **Example:** They have lived in the following countries: France, Germany, Spain, and Bulgaria.

1. The consumers' group tested the following vans Ford, Nissan, Toyota, and Chevrolet.

2. Samuel Clemens wrote under a name derived from his river pilot days Mark Twain.

3. A hospital needs more than doctors and nurses it also must have lab technicians, janitors, electricians, cooks, and so on.

4. Planted in the flower garden were crocuses, daffodils, hyacinths, and irises.

5. In modern times, several women have governed nations Golda Meir, Indira Gandhi, Margaret Thatcher, and Corazon Aquino are examples.

6. All students must take the following courses math, English, health, communications, history, and science.

7. After several burglaries, the tenants' association held an emergency meeting the group discussed security measures.

8. Eric Blair is better known by his pen name George Orwell.

9. The cost of bringing up children includes the following items housing, food, clothing, medical attention, and education.

10. Ten inches of snow fell last night the roads are impassable.

29 The Dash

Less formal than the colon, the **dash** gives emphasis or clarity to extra information in a sentence. Use a dash:

1. To separate an introductory series from its summarizing clause.
2. To emphasize a parenthetical element.
3. To clarify a parenthetical element containing commas.
4. To introduce a terminal element.

Nabokov, Borges, Castaneda—these were his favorite writers.

There was a frost—unbelievable as it seems—in August.

One teenage fad—puzzling to most adults, but especially to parents—was wearing sneakers with the laces untied.

The scarecrow in *The Wizard of Oz* was frightened of only one thing—a lighted match.

(See Exercise 29-1.)

EXERCISE 29-1   Dashes

Put dashes where necessary in the following sentences.

> ***Example:***   He hated only one thing—snakes.

1. Most European languages are related, with one notable exception Basque.

2. Edgar Allan Poe, Nathaniel Hawthorne, Herman Melville, Ralph Waldo Emerson, Henry David Thoreau these American authors wrote in the 19th century.

3. Thousands of lives were saved by one law the 55-mile-per-hour speed limit.

4. Coffee strange as it seems sometimes calms hyperactive children.

5. Three churches designed by Palladio the Redentore, the Zitelle, and San Giorgio are in the Italian city of Venice.

6. He is good at all board games except one chess.

7. Male seahorses not the females become pregnant.

8. The course will feature two science writers Lewis Thomas and Stephen Jay Gould.

9. In the past, only amateur athletes not professionals could compete in the Olympics.

10. Centuries ago, Europe was devastated by a single disease bubonic plague.

30 Parentheses

Parentheses enclose information that breaks the continuity of the sentence or paragraph. The information within parentheses may be omitted without changing the meaning of the sentence.

30a With Parenthetical Comments and Additional Information

Use parentheses to enclose information that you do not want to emphasize.

Down coats (which are bulky but lightweight) are extremely warm.

30b With Items in a Series

Use parentheses to enclose numerals and letters designating items in a series.

To keep the car running during freezing weather, one should (a) keep the gas tank full, (b) add dry gas, and (c) make sure the battery has a full charge.

30c With Other Punctuation Marks

Use a capital letter and a period for a parenthetical sentence that stands by itself, but not for a parenthetical sentence within another sentence.

Christina Rossetti is considered by many to be the greatest female poet in the English language. (She was the sister of the poet and painter, Dante Gabriel Rossetti.)
Three-wheeled recreational vehicles (these vehicles are especially popular with teenagers) have recently been banned.

A comma, semicolon, or colon should be placed *outside* a closing parenthesis.

Although New Zealand is not really near Australia (they are 1,200 miles apart), many people confuse the two nations.

A question mark or exclamation point is placed *inside* the closing parenthesis if the parenthetical words express a question or an exclamation. The question mark or exclamation point is placed *outside* the closing parenthesis if the main sentence is a question or an exclamation.

> Her weeks at Outward Bound (what an experience**!**) built her confidence and self-reliance.
>
> What are the best-known works of Edith Wharton (a 20th-century novelist**)?**

(See Exercise 31-1.)

31 Brackets

Use brackets:

1. To enclose information or editorial comments inserted into quotations.
2. To replace parentheses within parentheses.

"This sort of crime [arson] is destroying our town," said the mayor.

Her letter began, "Deer [sic] friend."

Picasso influenced generations of artists. (See pp. 100–105 [color plates] for examples of his major works.)

(See Exercise 31-1.)

EXERCISE 31-1   Brackets and Parentheses

Add parentheses and/or brackets where necessary in the following sentences.

> **Example:** He was in both World War I (1914–1918) and World War II (1939–1945).

1. The trumpeter swan, once nearly extinct, is making a comeback. (See page 56 [map for an analysis of nesting sites.

2. The editor was distressed to discover that the headline read, "Governor Apoligizes *sic* to Rural Community."

3. The housing bill for a related story, see page B8 was debated by the state legislature.

4. His doctor recommended that he do three things a lose weight, b stop smoking, and c get regular exercise.

5. Napoleon I 1769–1821 was born in Corsica.

6. He said that it was "an incredulous *sic* coincidence."

7. The oil spill see page 13 will greatly affect the area's ecology.

8. Marcus predicted, "In this event [1,300 meters I will set a new record."

9. While on vacation you can make your home look occupied by a leaving some lights on, b asking a neighbor to collect your mail, and c having a radio playing.

10. The proposed tuition increase see page 12 for a detailed analysis will affect thousands of students.

32 Quotation Marks

Quotation marks, which are always used in pairs, enclose quoted material and certain kinds of titles.

32a For Direct Quotations

Quotation marks enclose a direct quotation—the exact words of a speaker or writer.

> Adelle Davis writes, "The Harvard physicians also found that there were more infections among the babies whose mothers' diets had been poor."

When writing dialogue, start a new paragraph each time the speaker changes.

> "Where's the bus stop?" asked Harry.
> "It's two blocks north, just after the hardware store," replied Grace.
> "Thanks," said Harry.

32b For Quotations within Quotations

Use single quotation marks to enclose quoted material within another quotation.

> Mrs. Brisbon said, "I agree with the pediatrician Dr. Spock, who said, 'Don't be overawed by what the experts say.'"

32c For Titles of Short Works

Use quotation marks to enclose the quoted titles of short stories, short poems, one-act plays, essays, articles, subdivisions of books, episodes of a television series, songs, short musical compositions, and dissertations.

Henry James's short story "The Marriages" was written in 1891.

32d With Other Punctuation Marks

Place a comma or a period inside a closing quotation mark.

"The rain," said the weather forecaster, "will end tonight."

Place a semicolon or a colon outside a closing quotation mark.

Many anthologies contain E. M. Forster's famous essay "Mr. Wood"; in it, Forster discusses the evils of owning property.

Place a question mark or an exclamation point inside a closing quotation mark if the quotation itself is a question or exclamation.

The headline read "Who's in charge?"

Place a question mark or an exclamation point outside a closing quotation mark if the sentence is a question or exclamation but the quotation is not.

What famous advertisement says "I want you"?

32e Misused Quotation Marks

Do *not* use quotation marks in the following cases:

1. When quoting four or more lines of prose or poetry. Instead, indent and single-space.
2. When writing indirect quotations, which are not the *exact* words of a speaker or writer.
3. When writing the title (used as the heading) of your own paper, theme, or essay.

(See Exercises 32-1 and 32-2.)

EXERCISE 32-1 Quotation Marks

Put quotation marks where necessary in the following sentences. One sentence needs no quotation marks.

> **Example:** She insisted, "I do not need to go to the hospital."

1. Recalling childhood visits, Mark Twain said, It was a heavenly place for a boy, that farm of my uncle John's.

2. Ms. Reyes exclaimed, I disagree with the mayor when he claims, Our schools are functioning well.

3. The police officer reported that shots had been fired inside a savings bank.

4. Chapter 15 is titled Pediatric Medication.

5. T. S. Eliot's play *The Cocktail Party* is ostensibly the subject of Thurber's comic essay What Cocktail Party?

6. Generations of students have been amused by the essay A Modest Proposal by Jonathan Swift.

7. The dance critic wrote, The dancers were spirited and well trained; this comment pleased the ballet company's director.

8. Jessica asked, Do you agree with Freud's words, There are no accidents?

9. The team, said the coach yesterday, needs a good center.

10. The car won't start, said Lamont.
    Put it in park, replied Kelly, and try again.

EXERCISE 32-2 | Quotation Marks

Put quotation marks where necessary in the following sentences. One sentence needs no quotation marks.

> **Example:** The class read the essay "Shooting an Elephant."

1. In 1854 Thoreau delivered an address entitled Slavery in Massachusetts; in it, he deplored the returning of an escaped slave to Virginia.

2. Aylmer is a character in a short story called The Birthmark; he attempts to remove a small birthmark from his otherwise perfect wife.

3. Alexander Pope's poem Ode on Solitude was written when he was twelve years old.

4. In the 1988 Winter Olympics, said the sportscaster, one bobsled team was from Jamaica.

5. In regard to so-called woman's intuition, H. L. Mencken writes, Intuition? Bosh!

6. Have you read the chapter The Dying Whale?

7. Dan remarked, The old Coca-Cola slogan, It's the Real Thing, was very clever.

8. The well-known painting Aristotle Contemplating the Bust of Homer is in the Metropolitan Museum of Art.

9. The travel agent says that all the flights to Atlanta are full.

10. James Baldwin's essay Notes of a Native Son begins, On the 29th of July, in 1943, my father died.

33   Ellipsis Points

Ellipsis points are spaced periods used to indicate that part of a quotation has been omitted.

Use three ellipsis points within a quotation to show that part of the quotation has been omitted.

> Galsworthy describes a character thus: "She had quite a reputation for saying the wrong thing, and . . . she would hold to it when she had said it, and add to it another wrong thing, and so on."

Use a period and three ellipsis points to show that the end of a sentence has been left out of a quotation.

> Samuel Eliot Morrison writes: "Exploring American history has been a very absorbing and exciting business. . . . Thousands of graduate students have produced thousands of monographs on every aspect of the history of the Americas."

(See Exercise 33-1.)

EXERCISE 33-1 Ellipsis Points

On separate paper, rewrite each paragraph, omitting some words. Indicate omissions with ellipsis points.

1. As a child, W. E. B. DuBois attended Sunday school. He was particularly interested in the biblical story of Esau and Jacob, judging the latter unfavorably as a cad and a liar. Jacob, he felt, was an unsuitable hero.

2. Stephen Jay Gould, a teacher of biology and a research biologist at Harvard, has written many essays for the magazine *Natural History.* The subjects of his essays have included evolution, intelligence, and even Walt Disney's cartoon character Mickey Mouse.

3. January may seem, to those not in the know, to be an idle month for gardeners, but gardeners know different. In January seed catalogs arrive, most of them illustrated with color photographs. Enormous pumpkins, huge tomatoes, impossibly brilliant flowers—all entice the snowbound gardener longing for spring.

4. Eudora Welty, born in Mississippi in 1909, published her first collection of stories in 1941 and her first novel a year later. Her novel *The Optimist's Daughter,* published in 1972, won a Pulitzer Prize.

5. In his book *Language in Thought and Action,* S. I. Hayakawa writes that many Americans regard the dictionary as an authority, believing that every word has a correct meaning. A dictionary, on the contrary, is meant to be a "historian, not a lawgiver."

34 Underlining

Underlining, in a typed handwritten paper, highlights certain titles, words, or phrases and is used to indicate italics.

Underline the titles of books, full-length musical compositions, plays, long poems, and the names of newspapers, magazines, ships, boats, and aircraft.

> Tennessee Williams: A Tribute (*book*)
> Business Week (*magazine*)

Underline foreign words or phrases not commonly used in English.

> The name of an Italian dish, coda di rospo, does not denote its literal translation, "tail of toad."

Underline letters, words, or phrases being named.

> How many s's are in the word possesses?

Underline, sparingly, words and phrases for emphasis.

> You must stop smoking!

(See Exercise 34-1.)

EXERCISE 34-1 Italics

Underline where necessary in the following sentences.

> **Example:** She wants to see the new production of <u>Hamlet</u>.

1. This season she is singing the title roles in the operas Manon Lescaut and Madame Butterfly.

2. The expression je m'en fiche does not have an exact English translation.

3. He sometimes spells the word necessary with only one s.

4. She subscribes to Fortune, Forbes, Business Week, and The Wall Street Journal.

5. Never smoke while pumping gas.

6. The acting workshop did several scenes from Romeo and Juliet.

7. Little House on the Prairie and other books in the Laura Ingalls Wilder series have been read by several generations of children.

8. That remark was not necessary!

9. The word possesses has five s's.

10. Semper fidelis is the motto of the United States Marine Corps.

35 The Apostrophe

Apostrophes are used in possessive forms, in certain plural forms, in contractions, and for omissions.

35a In Possessive Forms

Add *'s* to form the possessive of singular nouns and of some indefinite pronouns.

> Shakespeare**'s** history plays are exciting, if not always accurate.
> Tennessee Williams**'s** play *The Glass Menagerie* opened in 1945.
> The quality of the environment should be everyone**'s** concern.

Add *'s* to form the possessive of a plural noun not ending in *s*.

> A pediatrician is a children**'s** doctor.

Add an apostrophe alone to form the possessive of a plural noun ending in *s*.

> The students**'** papers were piled on the desk.

To form the possessive of a compound noun, make the last word possessive.

> My brother-in-law**'s** apartment is being renovated.

To show joint possession, add *'s* to the last noun in a pair or series.

> Rodgers and Hammerstein**'s** musicals include *Oklahoma!* and *Carousel*.

To show individual possession, add *'s* to each noun in a pair or series.

> Brando**'s** and Olivier**'s** acting styles are quite different.

Do *not* use an apostrophe with possessive personal pronouns.

Her computer printer works more quietly than **yours.**

35b In Plural Forms

Add *'s* to form the plural of words being named, letters of the alphabet, abbreviations, numerals, and symbols.

Your essay is filled with too many therefore**'s.**
He received one A and two B**'s** on his last grade report.
The Depression lasted through the 1930**'s** (or 1930**s**).

35c In Contractions

Use an apostrophe to indicate a missing letter or letters in a contraction. (Use contractions in informal writing.)

Aren't you aware that it's raining?

In most formal writing, contractions should be avoided. They are used for the most part in speech and in informal writing.

FORMAL: When he died, Giacomo Puccini **had not** finished his opera *Turandot.*

INFORMAL: He **hadn't** picked up his mail in several days.

35d For Omissions

Use an apostrophe to show that part of a word or number has been omitted.

In '80 John Lennon's murder shocked the rock **'n'** roll world.

(See Exercises 35-1 through 35-3.)

EXERCISE 35-1   Apostrophes

Put *'s* or an apostrophe alone where necessary in the following sentences.

> ***Example:***   All the lights are on in the Senator*(s)* office.

1. Mr. Rojas daughter is an accountant.

2. The wild pitch hit the umpire face mask.

3. The vice president main duty is to preside over the Senate.

4. I decided to clean up Bill and Sam room.

5. Mark and Andy rooms are almost identically furnished.

6. The children coats are in the hall closet.

7. Milagros daughter is younger than yours.

8. The supervisor office isnt open yet, is it?

9. The show dogs coats were carefully washed and brushed.

10. In the 1920s, buying alcoholic beverages wasnt legal.

Name ______________________________

Score ______________

EXERCISE 35-2 Apostrophes

Put *'s* or an apostrophe alone where necessary in the following sentences.

Example:	The children('s) room is almost always messy.

1. She is always willing to consider her employees suggestions.
2. Penn and Teller comedy routines are hilarious.
3. He reverses all his bs and ds when he writes.
4. The meeting will take place in Dr. Santos office.
5. Its hard to believe that its nearly the end of the century.
6. Humans didnt walk on the moon until 69.
7. Dr. Brown and Dr. Carlucci diagnoses were quite similar.
8. Many women groups support the Equal Rights Amendment.
9. She always listens to her father-in-law opinions.
10. Mary short story was published in the school magazine.

EXERCISE 35-3 Apostrophes

Put *'s* or an apostrophe alone where necessary in the following sentences.

> ***Example:***   Mrs. Rojas room is at the end of the hall.

1. The chairperson speech was short but informative.

2. His presentation was spoiled by too many *you know*.

3. The men room is down the hall on the right.

4. The technician poured 20ccs of liquid into the test tube.

5. The girls locker room needs a new floor.

6. One doesnt think of Waxahachie, Texas as a center of acting, but in the 70s and 80s dozens of movies were filmed there.

7. Nabokov most notorious novel is *Lolita*.

8. A Mexican ranch owner has bred a cow that one-quarter normal size.

9. John Williams music was used in the movie *Star Wars*.

10. Its true that Michael Jackson owns the rights to most of Lennon and McCartney music.

36 The Hyphen

36a In Compound Nouns

Most compound nouns are written either as one word or as two separate words, rather than with a hyphen. Hyphens are used in compound nouns when (1) the two nouns are of equal importance or (2) the compound noun has three or more words.

philosopher-king
son-in-law

Use a dictionary to check whether a compound word needs a hyphen.

36b In Compound Adjectives

Hyphenate two or more words serving as a single adjective before a noun. Do not hyphenate these words when they follow a noun.

an ill-tempered man
a man who is ill tempered

a medical-school degree
a degree from a medical school

Do not hyphenate two or more words preceding a noun when the first word ends in *-ly*.

an expertly tailored jacket
a poorly designed automobile

Use a "hanging" hyphen in a series where part of the compound adjective is implied.

only the third- and fourth-year medical students

36c In Compound Numbers and Fractions

Hyphenate spelled-out numbers from twenty-one through ninety-nine and spelled-out fractions used as adjectives.

twenty-three students
ninety-seven dollars
a two-thirds success rate

36d With Prefixes and Suffixes

Hyphens are not generally used between roots and their prefixes and suffixes. However, note the following exceptions.

re-create (*to remake*)
re-elect (*hyphen between two identical vowels*)
all-star
ex-wife
mayor-elect

36e For Word Division at the End of a Line

A hyphen is used to show that a word has been divided at the end of a line. Here are some general rules for word division. Consult a dictionary for words not covered here. Words should be divided:

1. Between syllables.

re-fine

2. Between double consonants.

dif-ferent

3. Between a root and its prefix or suffix.

dis-interested

4. At the hyphen in a hyphenated word.

self-winding

Do *not* divide proper names or one-syllable words. Do *not* divide a word so that a one-letter syllable or two-letter suffix appears on a separate line. (See Exercises 36-1 through 36-3.)

EXERCISE 36-1   Hyphens

Choose the correct form in each of the following sentences.

> ***Example:***   (~~One-half~~, ⟨One half⟩) of these people voted in the primary, but a (⟨One-half⟩, ~~one half~~) turnout is quite poor.

1. She reached the (*quarter-final, quarter final*) of the tennis tournament after a (*hard-fought, hard fought*) match.

2. His (*even-tempered, even tempered*) manner calmed the restless audience.

3. (*Blood-thirsty, Bloodthirsty*) growls could be heard in the (*back-ground, background*).

4. Your article was (*thought-provoking, thought provoking*), and it impressed your (*class-mates, classmates*).

5. The (*rapidly-falling, rapidly falling*) dollar alarmed my (*daughter-in-law, daughter in law*), who is a banker.

6. This building contains the (*first-, first*), (*second-, second*), and (*third-, third*) grade classrooms.

7. (*Seventy-five, Seventy five*) people answered the advertisement.

8. (*One-fourth, One fourth*) of those contacted responded to the poll; a (*one-fourth, one fourth*) response is considered excellent.

9. The (*governor-elect, governor elect*) will not answer questions about her (*ex-husband, ex husband*).

10. I have a (*bird's-eye, bird's eye*) view of the garden, where (*black-eyed, black eyed*) daisies are in bloom.

EXERCISE 36-2 | Hyphens

Choose the correct form in each of the following sentences.

> **Example:** She is a (~~law-school~~, ~~law school~~) graduate.

1. The (*long-suffering, long suffering*) businessperson listened to his partner's wild description of a "sure" (*money-maker, money maker*).

2. A (*blue-eyed, blue eyed*) kitten played in the (*pet-shop, pet shop*) window.

3. The (*club-house, clubhouse*) is contructed of (*rough-hewn, rough hewn*) logs.

4. She plays tennis (*left-handed, left handed*) but writes with her right hand.

5. This nursing home offers both (*short-, short*) and (*long-term, long term*) care.

6. (*Increasingly-heavy, Increasingly heavy*) taxes have burdened the (*hard-pressed, hard pressed*) middle class.

7. The (*all-star, all star*) soccer player scored a (*last-minute, last minute*) goal.

8. She developed (*twenty-five, twenty five*) rolls of film in the school's (*dark-room, darkroom*).

9. The child's behavior was (*too-good-to-be-true, too good to be true*).

10. A (*one-tenth, one tenth*) increase in profits was (*long-expected, long expected*).

| EXERCISE 36-3 | Hyphens for Line Breaks |

Write each of the following words with a hyphen to indicate where the word should be divided at the end of a line. Not every word can be divided.

| **Example:** smelling | _____ *smell-ing* _____ |

1. deceptive _____

2. nibble _____

3. accurate _____

4. evolution _____

5. convince _____

6. absolute _____

7. William _____

8. evince _____

9. prism _____

10. careless _____

11. fetter _____

12. inconsistent _____

13. massive _____

14. supersacral _____

15. Hawthorne _____

16. polyglot _____

17. misleading _____

18. dishonor _____

19. walked   _____

20. caption   _____

37 The Slash, Abbreviations, Numbers

37a The Slash

Use a slash to indicate that one or both words in a pair may be selected.

He wants to play football and/or basketball.

Use a slash to indicate the end of a line of poetry when you are not using the block form of citation.

John Donne's poem begins: "I am two fools, I know, / For loving, and for saying so / In whining poetry."

Avoid the construction s/he, a nonstandard usage for *she and he.*

37b Abbreviations

The following abbreviations are acceptable in formal writing.

1. Certain designations preceding names:

Mr.	Messrs.	St. or Ste.
Ms.	Mmes.	Mt.
Mrs.	Dr.	

2. A designation or academic degree following a name:

Jr.	Esq.	M.D.
Sr.	B.A.	D.D.S.

3. Initials and acronyms for well-known organizations and governmental agencies:

CIA   OPEC
NRC   YMCA

4. Indicators of time and dates:

A.D.   A.M. (*or* a.m.)
B.C.   P.M. (*or* p.m.)

5. Common Latin words and expressions:

c. *or* ca. ("about")   etc. ("and others," "and so on")
cf. ("compare")   i.e. ("that is")
e.g. ("for example")   viz. ("namely")

Abbreviations are not acceptable in the following cases.

1. Spell out most designations preceding names:

INCORRECT: Prof. Smith
CORRECT: Professor Smith

INCORRECT: Pres. Taft
CORRECT: President Taft

2. Spell out the names of days and months:

INCORRECT: The second Tues. in Nov.
CORRECT: The second Tuesday in November

3. Spell out the names of cities, states, and countries:

INCORRECT: He works in Boston, Ma.
CORRECT: He works in Boston, Massachusetts.

4. Spell out first names:

INCORRECT: Thom. Edison held more than 1,300 patents.
CORRECT: Thomas Edison held more than 1,300 patents.

5. Spell out the words *Brothers, Corporation,* and *Company* in names of businesses (except in addresses or bibliographical information):

INCORRECT: She works for the Xerox Corp.
CORRECT: She works for the Xerox Corporation.

6. In formal, nontechnical writing, spell out units of measurement:

INCORRECT: The baby weighs 7 lbs.
CORRECT: The baby weighs seven pounds.

In technical writing, however, abbreviations are acceptable and often preferred.

37c Numbers

In formal, nontechnical writing, use numbers only in specific instances.

When *not* to use numbers

1. Never begin a sentence with a number. Spell out the number:

Eighty-six customers asked for refunds.

2. Spell out all numbers that can be rewritten as one or two words and that modify a noun:

The designer used **thirty-two** yards of tulle in this costume.

When to use numbers

1. Use numbers when they cannot be written as one or two words:

For this opinion poll, **950** people were interviewed.

2. Use numbers for decimals or mixed numbers:

The Berkshires got **10½** inches of rain this month.

3. Use numbers for street addresses:

905 West **115th** Street

4. Use numbers for page numbers, percentages, degrees, and amounts of money with the symbols $ and ¢:

The article on **page 17** states that **40%** of the voters have no preference.

5. Use numbers for dates and for hours expressed with A.M. or P.M.:

The meeting is scheduled for **10 A.M.** on January **28.**

6. Use numbers with units of measurement:

The garden measures **20'** by **30'.**

7. Use numbers for numbers in a series:

For a week, the runner recorded the miles she had run each day: **3, 4, 3, 5, 3.5, 3.5, 5.**

8. Use numbers for identification numbers:

Flight **585** has just landed.

9. When one number immediately follows another, spell out the first and use a number for the second:

For this project, I need **four 5**-foot planks.

(See Exercises 37-1 and 37-2.)

EXERCISE 37-1   Abbreviations, Contractions, and Numbers

Choose the correct form in each of the following sentences.

> ***Example:***   (~~Prof.~~, *Professor*) Norton will arrive on Flight (~~46~~, ~~forty-six~~).

1. The speaker, (*Prof.*, *Professor*) Wright, was introduced by John Beatty, (*Jr.* *Junior*).

2. Each person can choose the schedule (*s/he, she or he*) prefers.

3. Only (*1½, one and a half*) inches of snow fell in (*Nev., Nevada*).

4. Flight (*602, six hundred two*) will arrive at (*9:30, nine-thirty*) P.M.

5. Thanksgiving is celebrated on the fourth (*Thurs., Thursday*) of (*Nov., November*).

6. (*Dr., Doctor*) Gillis worked for the Rand (*Corp., Corporation*) for (*10, ten*) years.

7. The baby, named (*Benj., Benjamin*) Miller, weighed eleven (*lbs., pounds*) at the age of (*2, two*) months.

8. (*350, Three hundred fifty*) people were on Flight (*403, four hundred three*) to Madrid.

9. Inches of rain recorded in the last four days were as follows: (*1, ½, 0, and ½; one, one half, zero, and one half*).

10. Even a small (*10' by 10', ten foot by ten foot*) garden can yield many (*lbs., pounds*) of vegetables.

EXERCISE 37-2   The Slash, Abbreviations, and Numbers

Choose the correct form in each of the following sentences.

> **Example:**   (~~Wm.~~, William) Reed was born in (1940, ~~nineteen hundred and forty~~).

1. The address of the Jackson (*Co.*, *Company*) is (*59*, *fifty-nine*) North Street, Waterville, (*Penn.*, *Pennsylvania*).

2. I need (*2*, *two*) (*6*, *six*)-foot extension cords.

3. The Louisiana Purchase was authorized by (*Pres.*, *President*) Jefferson in (*1803*, *eighteen hundred and three*).

4. The editorial on page (*41*, *forty-one*) claims that nearly (*20*, *twenty*) percent of the town's high school students drop out.

5. The typewriter costs (*$385*, *three hundred eighty-five dollars*).

6. (*16*, *Sixteen*) fluid ounces make (*1*, *one*) pint, and two pints make a (*qt.*, *quart*).

7. Paula Smith, (*M.D.*, *Doctor of Medicine*), is chief of surgery at (*Conn.*, *Connecticut*) Hospital.

8. He used (*8½*, *eight and a half*) pounds of strawberries to make several quarts of jam.

9. (*Sen.*, *Senator*) Green has appointed (*Rob't.*, *Robert*) Griffin as her press secretary.

10. Anna wants to study law (*and or*, *and/or*) economics.

PART VI

SPELLING

38 Spelling Accurately

38a Doubling the Final Consonant

Following are guidelines for doubling the consonant when adding suffixes to words that end in a consonant-vowel-consonant (c-v-c) combination.

Double the final consonant of a one-syllable c-v-c word when adding a suffix that begins with a vowel.

> put + ing = pu**tt**ing
> mop + ed = mo**pp**ed
> stop + er = sto**pp**er

Doubling the consonant maintains the short vowel sound in the root word.

When adding a suffix beginning with a vowel to a c-v-c word of more than one syllable, double the consonant if the accent falls on the word's last syllable.

> expél + ed = expé**ll**ed
> begín + ing = begí**nn**ing
> refér + ed = refé**rr**ed

When adding a suffix beginning with a vowel to a c-v-c word or more than one syllable, do not double the consonant if the accent shifts to the first syllable when the suffix is added.

> refér + ence = réfe**r**ence
> prefér + ence = préfe**r**ence

When adding a suffix beginning with a vowel to a c-v-c word of more than one syllable, do not double the final consonant if the accent does not fall on the last syllable.

fálter + ed = fáltered
énter + ing = éntering

Do not double the final consonant of a c-v-c word when the suffix added begins with a consonant.

fit   + ness = fitness
ship + ment = shipment

Do not double the final consonant in any word that does not end in a c-v-c combination.

shriek   + ing = shrieking
pretend + er   = pretender

(See Exercises 38-1 through 38-3.)

38b Dropping the Silent *e*

Drop the silent *e* when adding most suffixes beginning with a vowel.

hate   + ing = hating
write   + er   = writer
pleasure + able = pleasurable
trace   + ed   = traced

Exceptions

hoe + ing = hoeing
mile + age = mileage

When adding *-able* or *-ous,* keep the silent *e* if the letter *e* is preceded by the letter *c* or *g.*

change + able = changeable
courage + ous = courageous

Keep the silent *e* when adding a suffix beginning with a consonant.

hope + ful = hopeful
care + less = careless
wise + ly   = wisely

Exceptions

argue + ment = argument
judge + ment = judgment
true   + ly   = truly

(See Exercises 38-4 and 38-5.)

38c Changing *y* to *i*

Change *y* to *i* when adding most suffixes if the letter *y* is preceded by a consonant.

hap**py** + er   = happ**i**er
stu**dy** + ed   = stud**i**ed
love**ly** + ness = lovel**i**ness
lone**ly** + ness = lonel**i**ness

Exceptions

dry + ly   = dryly
shy + ness = shyness

Do not change *y* to *i* when adding *-ing* or *-ist*.

marry + ing = marrying
study + ing = studying
copy   + ist   = copyist
try   + ing = trying

Do not change *y* to *i* when adding a suffix if the letter *y* is preceded by a vowel.

play   + ing = playing
destroy + er   = destroyer
delay   + ed   = delayed
essay   + ist   = essayist

Exceptions

pay + ed = paid
say + ed = said

(See Exercises 38-6 and 38-7.)

38d Choosing between *ie* and *ei*

In most caes, place *i* before *e* except after *c*. Place *e* before *i* when the two letters together are pronounced as *ā* (as in *weigh*).

i *BEFORE* **e**

believe   view
niece   pierce

e *BEFORE* **i** *AFTER* **c**

receive   ceiling
deceive   perceive

PRONOUNCED AS **ā**

neighbor   reign
weigh   vein

EXCEPTIONS

either   heir
seize   height
leisure   weird
neither

The rule does not apply when the two letters are pronounced as parts of separate syllables.

deity   society

(See Exercise 38-8.)

38e Forming Noun Plurals

Add *s* to the singular to form the plural of most nouns.

photograph   photograph**s**
computer   computer**s**

Add *s* to the singular to form the plural of nouns ending in *y* preceded by a vowel.

donkey   donkey**s**
delay   delay**s**

Change *y* to *i* and add *-es* to form the plural of nouns (except proper nouns) ending in *y* preceded by a consonant.

tendency   tendenc**ies**
country   countr**ies**

Add *-es* to the singular to form the plural of nouns ending in *s, ch, sh, x,* or *z.*

dress   dress**es**
church   church**es**
tax   tax**es**

Add *s* to the singular to form the plural of nouns ending in *o* preceded by a vowel.

trio   trio**s**
radio   radio**s**
video   video**s**

Add either *s* or *-es* to form the plural of nouns ending in *o* preceded by a consonant.

ADD s

piano   piano**s**
memo   memo**s**

ADD es

hero   hero**es**
echo   echo**es**

ADD s OR es

flamingo   flamingo**s** *or* flamingo**es**
cargo   cargo**s** *or* cargo**es**

Add *s* to form the plural of most nouns ending in *f* or *fe* and of all nouns ending in *ff.*

belief   belief**s**
safe   safe**s**
staff   staff**s**

However, for some nouns ending in *f* or *fe,* form the plural by changing *f* or *fe* to *v* and adding *s.*

USE -ves

knife	kni**ves**
wife	wi**ves**
life	li**ves**

USE S OR ves

dwarf	dwarf**s** *or* dwar**ves**
scarf	scarf**s** *or* scar**ves**
wharf	wharf**s** *or* whar**ves**

For compound nouns written as one word, form the plural by applying the preceding rules to the end of the compound.

cupful	cupful**s**
housewife	housewi**ves**
soapbox	soapbox**es**

EXCEPTION

passerby	passer**s**by

For compound nouns in which the words are joined by a hyphen or written separately, make the chief word plural.

father-in-law	father**s**-in-law
runner-up	runner**s**-up
grade school	grade school**s**
video camera	video camera**s**

Add *'s* to the singular to form the plural of numbers, letters, symbols, and words being named.

5**'s**	if**'s**
b**'s**	maybe**'s**

Add *s* or *-es* to form the plural of proper nouns.

Wednesday**s**
the Davis**es**

Do *not* add *s* to irregular plural forms (except those in which singular *-is* becomes plural *-es*).

child	children	mouse	mice
man	men	alumnus	alumni
woman	women	radius	radii
ox	oxen	foot	feet
louse	lice	tooth	teeth

BUT

analysis	analyses
crisis	crises

Some nouns have the same form for both singular and plural.

deer	species
salmon	series
trout	moose
sheep	

(See Exercise 38-9.)

Name _____

Score _____

EXERCISE 38-1   Doubling the Final Consonant

Add *-ing* to each of the following words, doubling the final consonant where necessary.

> **Example:** trip   *tripping* _____

1. shop   _____
2. admit   _____
3. crawl   _____
4. get   _____
5. put   _____
6. eat   _____
7. stop   _____
8. develop   _____
9. expel   _____
10. occur   _____
11. rob   _____
12. clear   _____
13. begin   _____
14. grip   _____
15. prefer   _____

Name _____

Score _____

EXERCISE 38-2   Doubling the Final Consonant

Add *-ed* to each of the following words, doubling the final consonant where necessary.

> **Example:** fan   *fanned* _____

1. permit   _____

2. repel   _____

3. dot   _____

4. snap   _____

5. succeed   _____

6. prefer   _____

7. trip   _____

8. intend   _____

9. deter   _____

10. abandon   _____

11. defer   _____

12. trap   _____

13. faint   _____

14. wrap   _____

15. lean   _____

EXERCISE 38-3 Doubling the Final Consonant

Add each indicated suffix, doubling the final consonant where necessary.

> **Example:** ship + ed = *shipped* _____

1. slip + er = _____

2. retain + er = _____

3. chop + ing = _____

4. prefer + ence = _____

5. occur + ence = _____

6. hat + ful = _____

7. rob + ing = _____

8. claim + ed = _____

9. wet + ness = _____

10. pit + ed = _____

11. train + ed = _____

12. forget + ful = _____

13. hop + ed = _____

14. regret + ing = _____

15. shop + ing = _____

EXERCISE 38-4   Dropping the Silent *e*

Add each indicated suffix, dropping the silent *e* where necessary.

> **Example:**   engage + ing =   *engaging* _____

1. entrance + ing =   _____

2. place + ed =   _____

3. taste + ing =   _____

4. hope + ful =   _____

5. escape + ing =   _____

6. whine + ing =   _____

7. judge + ment =   _____

8. peace + ful =   _____

9. dine + er =   _____

10. rage + ed =   _____

11. hate + ing =   _____

12. change + ed =   _____

13. care + ful =   _____

14. hinge + ing =   _____

15. robe + er =   _____

EXERCISE 38-5   Dropping the Silent *e*

Add each indicated suffix, dropping the silent *e* where necessary.

Example: base + less =	*baseless* _____

1. engage + ed =   _____

2. transpose + ing =   _____

3. argue + ment =   _____

4. complete + ly =   _____

5. mile + age =   _____

6. deceive + er =   _____

7. cure + able =   _____

8. defense + ible =   _____

9. receive + ing =   _____

10. strive + ing =   _____

11. sure + ly =   _____

12. defense + ive =   _____

13. care + ful =   _____

14. live + ing =   _____

15. whine + ing =   _____

EXERCISE 38-6 Changing *y* to *i*

Add each indicated suffix, changing *y* to *i* where necessary.

> ***Example:*** study + ing = *studying* _____

1. study + ed =   _____

2. roomy + er =   _____

3. pay + ed =   _____

4. happy + ness =   _____

5. marry + ed =   _____

6. worry + er =   _____

7. dry + ly =   _____

8. marry + ing =   _____

9. likely + hood =   _____

10. lonely + ness =   _____

11. cry + ing =   _____

12. silly + est =   _____

13. pray + ed =   _____

14. hazy + er =   _____

15. fry + ed =   _____

EXERCISE 38-7   Changing *y* to *i*

Add each indicated suffix, changing *y* to *i* where necessary.

> ***Example:*** copy + ed =   *copied* _____

1. rely + ing =   _____

2. hazy + est =   _____

3. rally + ed =   _____

4. study + ing =   _____

5. copy + ist =   _____

6. play + ing =   _____

7. happy + er =   _____

8. lazy + ness =   _____

9. pray + ed =   _____

10. mortify + ed =   _____

11. stay + ing =   _____

12. testify + ing =   _____

13. shy + ed =   _____

14. marry + ed =   _____

15. carry + ed =   _____

EXERCISE 38-8   Choosing *ei* or *ie*

Choose the correct spelling in each of the following sentences.

> **Example:**   I never (received, recieved) your letter.

1. My little (*niece, neice*) does not (*believe, beleive*) the earth is round.

2. The queen (*riegned, reigned*) for forty years.

3. (*Niether, Neither*) of my (*nieghbors, neighbors*) is home.

4. The (*cieling, ceiling*) cannot hold the (*wieght, weight*) of such a heavy chandelier.

5. He (*fiegned, feigned*) illness to avoid going to work.

6. Working mothers have little (*liesure, leisure*) time.

7. The (*hieght, height*) of the new building being constructed will ruin our (*view, veiw*).

8. The movie was (*wierd, weird*) but funny.

9. A (*piercing, peircing*) whistle filled the air.

10. The lines of trees form a (*shield, sheild*) against the wind.

EXERCISE 38-9   Noun Plurals

Write the plural form of each of the following words.

Example:	son-in-law	*sons-in-law* _____

1. indication   _____

2. donkey   _____

3. theory   _____

4. desk   _____

5. tax   _____

6. radio   _____

7. potato   _____

8. staff   _____

9. self   _____

10. man   _____

11. child   _____

12. shelf   _____

13. tablespoon   _____

14. son-in-law   _____

15. high school   _____

16. mouse   _____

17. fuse   _____

18. shield   _____

19. deer   _____

20. tooth   _____

39 Troublesome Words

The following words are often misspelled, either by omitting necessary letters or by adding unneeded letters. The troublesome part or parts of each word are in **boldface.**

abando**n**ed
a**c**ademic
academic**ally**
a**cc**elerator
acce**p**table
a**cc**essible
a**cc**identa**l**ly
a**cc**o**mm**odate
a**cc**ompanied
a**cc**ompanying
a**cc**omplish
a**cc**umulate
a**cc**uracy
a**cc**ustomed
achie**v**ement
acknowle**dg**e
acknowledgment (no *e* after *g*)
a**c**quaintance
a**c**quire
a**c**quit
acreage
a**c**ross
actua**lly**
a**dd**ress
admi**ss**ion
admi**tt**ance
adoles**c**ent
advantag**e**ous
advertis**e**ment
a**e**rial

a**gg**ravate
a**gg**ressive
aisle
allo**tt**ing
a**l**most
a**l**ready
a**l**together
a**l**ways
amat**eu**r
among (no *u* after *o*)
a**m**ount
a**n**alysis
a**n**alyze
ancestry (no *a* after *t*)
a**nn**ihilate
a**nn**ouncement
a**nn**ual
a**n**other
a**p**artment
a**p**ologetically
a**p**ology
a**pp**aratus
a**pp**arent
a**pp**earance
a**pp**lies
a**pp**oint
a**pp**reciate
a**pp**ropriate
a**pp**ropriately
a**pp**roximate

385

approximately
arctic
arguing (no *e* after *u*)
argument (no *e* after *u*)
aspirin
assassination
association
atheist
athlete (no *e* after *h*)
athletic (no *e* after *h*)
attitude
awful (no *e* after *w*)
bankruptcy
bargain
basically
battalion
beautiful
becoming
before
beginning
benefited
biggest
biscuit
biting
boundary
bracelet
bulletin
business
calendar
camouflage
candidate
career
carrying
challenge
changeable
channel
characteristics
chocolate
chosen (no *o* after *o*)
clothes
column
coming
commercial
commission
commitment
committee
communism
communists

compel
compelled
competition
completely
conceivable (no *e* after *v*)
condemn
conferred
confused
connoisseur
conscience
conscientious
consists
continuous
controlled
controlling
controversial
convenient
coolly
criticism
crowded
cruelty (no *i* after *l*)
curriculum
dealt
decision
decorate
deferred
define
definitely
definition
descend
desirable (no *e* after *r*)
desperate
develop (no *e* after *p*)
diarrhea
different
dilemma
dilettante
dining
disagree
disappear
disappoint
disapprove
disaster
disastrous (no *e* after *t*)
discipline
discussion
dispel
dissatisfied

disservice
dissipate
distinct
drunkenness
during
ecstasy
efficiency
efficient
eliminate
embarrass
eminent
empty
endeavor
enemy
enthusiastically
entirely
entrance (no *e* after *t*)
environment
equipment (no *t* after *p*)
equipped
especially
essential
everything
exaggerate
excellent
excess
exercise (no *c* after *x*)
exhaustion
exhibition
exhilarate
existence (no *h* after *x*)
experience
explanation (no *i* after *l*)
extremely
fallacy
familiar
family
fascinate
fascism
favorite
February
fiery
final (no *i* after *n*)
financially
fission
fluorine
foreign
foresee

forfeit (no *e* after *r*)
forty (no *e* after *r*)
forward (no *e* after *r*)
fourth
frantically
fulfill
gaiety
generally
genius (no *o* after *i*)
government
grammatically
grievous (no *i* after *v*)
gruesome
guarantee
guerrilla
handicapped
handkerchief
harass
height (no *h* after *t*)
hemorrhage
heroes
hindrance (no *e* after *d*)
holiday
hopeless
hurriedly
hygiene
hypocrite
ideally
illogical
imagine
imitate
immediately
immense
impossible
incidentally
indispensable (no *e* after *s*)
individually
ingenious
initially
initiative
innocent
innocuous
inoculate
intellectual
intelligence
intelligent
interest
interfered

interference
interrupt
iridescent
irrelevant
irresistible
irritable
jewelry (no *e* after *l*)
judgment (no *e* after *g*)
knowledge
laboratory
larynx
later
laundry (no *e* after *d*)
lenient
liable
liaison
library
lightning (no *e* after *t*)
likely
listening
literature
loneliness
lonely
magazine
maintenance
manageable
maneuver
manner
manual
marriage
marriageable
mathematics
meanness
meant
medicine
medieval
mileage
millennium
miniature
miscellaneous
mischievous (no *i* after *v*)
missile
misspelled
mortgage
muscle
narrative
naturally
necessary

necessity
nineteen
ninety
ninth (no *e* after *in*)
noticeable
nowadays
nuisance
numerous
occasion
occasionally
occurred
occurrence
official
omission
omit
omitted
operate
opinion
opponent
opportunity
opposite
oppression
outrageous
pageant
pamphlet (no *e* after *h*)
panicked
paraffin
parallel
parliament
particular
pastime
peaceable
peculiar
permissible
picnicked
planned
playwright
pneumonia
pollute
Portuguese
possess
possession
possible
practically
preference
preferred
prejudiced
primitive

privilege (no *d* after *le*)
probably (no *a* after *ab*)
procedure (no *e* after *ce*)
profession
professor
pronunciation (no *o* after *on*)
psalm
psychology
ptomaine
publicly (no *al* after *c*)
pumpkin
quantity
quarrel
questionnaire
realize
rebellion
recession
recommend
reference
referring
relative
remember
remembrance (no *e* after *b*)
reminisce
remittance
restaurant
rhythm
roommate
saccharine
safety
satellite
scientists
scintillate
sergeant
shepherd
sheriff
shining
shrubbery
similar (no *i* after *l*)
sincerely
skiing
sophomore
souvenir
specifically
statistics (no *s* after *a*)
strenuous
stretch
stubbornness

studying
subtle
succeed
success
succession
sufficient
summary
summation
summed
supposed
suppress
surely
surrounding
swimming
syllable
symmetric
tariff
temperament
temperature
therefore
thorough
tobacco
tomorrow
transferred
trespass
truly (no *e* after *u*)
tyranny
unconscious
uncontrollable
undoubtedly
unmistakably (no *e* after *k*)
unnatural
unnecessary
until
used
useful
usually
vacuum
valuable
various
vaudeville
vegetable
vehicle
vengeance
villain
violence
warring
where

w**h**ether   w**ho**se
w**h**istle   wri**t**ing
who**ll**y   wri**tt**en

The following is a list of other words that are often misspelled.

abundant	eligible	performance
acre	emphasize	permanent
against	espionage	perseverance
a lot	exuberant	perspiration
anonymous	financier	phenomenon
arithmetic	galaxy	physician
article	guidance	pigeon
attendance	hers	poison
ballet	hospital	predominate
beggar	hundred	prescription
behavior	hypocrisy	prestige
believe	idiomatic	prevalent
beneficial	imagery	proceed
bibliography	incredible	propaganda
blasphemy	independent	propagate
boulevard	inevitable	pursue
buffet	insurance	pursuit
bureaucrat	interpretation	repetition
burial	involve	ridiculous
buried	January	sacrifice
carburetor	leisurely	salary
caricature	license	schedule
catalogue	liquor	secretary
catastrophe	luxurious	seize
category	magnificent	seizure
cellar	malicious	separate
cemetery	martyrdom	siege
children	mediocre	significance
circumstantial	melancholy	source
colossal	minuscule	specimen
comparative	minute	speech
complexion	naive	supersede
counselor	neurotic	surprise
courtesy	nickel	susceptible
criticize	nuclear	technical
debacle	nucleus	technique
despicable	ogre	tendency
detrimental	optimism	theirs
dictionary	ours	themselves
diphtheria	paid	tolerance
doesn't	paralysis	tortoise
eighth	penicillin	tragedy

tried	vigilance	yacht
Tuesday	vinegar	yours
unscrupulous	Wednesday	zinc
versatile	woman	

(See Exercises 39-1 through 39-5.)

EXERCISE 39-1 | Spelling

In each pair of sentences, circle the correct spelling. Cross out and correct the misspelling.

Example: She is a (professor) of astronomy.

                                        professor

I have to talk to my history ~~proffesor~~.

---

1. Someone abandoned a car near the railroad station.

   He found an abadoned puppy in the street.

2. Your neighborhood and mine are quite diferent.

   To get a thicker line, you must use a different pen.

3. In January she spent two days in the hopital.

   Hospital stays for most patients are shorter today than in the past.

4. She was dissatisfied with her life.

   A disatisfied person cannot work well.

5. They were truly astonished at their good luck.

   The blazing comet atonished astronomers.

6. There are several resturants on this block.

   Ms. McCoy manages a restaurant.

7. Salespeople often keep a log of their daily mileage.

   This car's gas milage is average.

8. Most of the goverment offices are downtown.

   The editorial criticized several government policies.

9. Amanda was born on February 15.

   Valentine's Day is Febuary 14.

10. She approaches challenges with a positive atitude.

    The models posed in awkward, contorted attitudes.

EXERCISE 39-2   Spelling

In each pair of sentences, circle the correct spelling. Cross out and correct the misspelling.

1. The coincidence is so unlikely as to be incredable.

   No one believed his incredible story.

2. Viewers are invited to call the television station to express their opionions.

   In my opinion, you should look for a more interesting job.

3. In her first job she acquired many skills.

   With careful investments he had aquired a small fortune.

4. The poem consits of five stanzas.

   Her science project consists of a model and a written description.

5. Can intelligence really be measured in standardized tests?

   I believe the ability to adapt is a sign of inteligence.

6. The canidate is holding a rally tonight.

   Do you want to hear the candidate speak?

7. After an illness, bedrest is beneficial.

   Exercise is benefical for almost everyone.

8. A loud arguement broke out in the street.

   The lawyer presented her closing argument.

9. Fire facinates most young children.

   Trains and trucks fascinate the little boy.

10. Do you think he is guilty or innocent?

    He claims that he is inocent.

EXERCISE 39-3 | Spelling

In each pair of sentences, circle the correct spelling. Cross out and correct the misspelling.

1. The old furnace is not efficient.

   An eficent kitchen has no wasted space.

2. The meeting started latter than I had hoped it would.

   We will discuss that issue later.

3. He has a tedency to procrastinate.

   The car has a tendency to pull to the left.

4. Too much praise will embarrass him.

   Reports of his alleged alcohol problem certainly did embarass the congressman.

5. All seniors in this school must take a hygeine course.

   Good public sanitation and personal hygiene prevent the spread of disease.

6. Some holidays have become very commerical.

   The movie was interrupted by many commercials.

7. The referee seperated the two boxers.

   In the crowd the child became separated from her mother.

8. She accidentally left her car headlights on.

   That mistake was made on purpose, not accidently.

9. Cries of ecstasy rang out as the children rushed toward the swimming pool.

   Winning the lottery has left them in ectasy.

10. The elderly actor is writting his memoirs.

    All prospective employees must take math and writing tests.

EXERCISE 39-4 Spelling in Brief Paragraphs

Correct the misspellings in the following items.

1. Finding his wife unconsious on the floor, he shouted a desparate cry for help. Luckily a neighbor trained in first aid heard him, so a tradgedy was averted.

2. Her accepting the job depends on weather it is satisfying intellectually rather than finacially. She is not interested in a high-salaried job that does not furfill her expectations.

3. The college offers four acadamic scholarships every year. To see if you are elegible for one of them, check the rules in the annual bulliten.

4. Stuborness is characteristic of two-year-old children. Although parents often find such behaviour unaceptable, it is completely normal.

5. The snowstorm was more than a niusance; it caused paralisys in the city, in great part because there was not a suffecent number of trucks and plows.

6. The Cloisters certainly does posess a wonderful collection of medeival art. In addition, it is located in a magnifacent setting in upper Manhattan.

7. The actor's interpetation of Hamlet displeased theater critics, who disliked his allmost continous glowering and frowning.

8. Luisa is an organized women who makes lists and keeps her calandar updated. She says that otherwise she would never remeber everything she has to do.

9. His perfrence is to live in the country where he claims noisy neighbors cannot harrass him. I think he exagerates the disadvantages of urban life.

10. The comittee plans to acumulate date on mortality rates in the city hospitals. Their report will analyse deaths in various catagories.

EXERCISE 39-5 Writing with Troublesome Words

On separate paper, write brief paragraphs using the suggested words.

> **Example:** surprise, among, tired
>
> *Lupe had hoped to run a good marathon, but to her surprise and delight she found herself among the first ten finishers. At the end she was tired but extremely pleased.*

1. marriage, believe, interest

2. definitely, permanent, necessary

3. violence, competitive, athlete

4. genius, imitate, planned

5. curriculum, succeed, omitted

6. beginning, environment, recommend

7. judgment, criticized, individual

8. familiar, occasionally, loneliness

9. individually, opportunity, amount

10. abandoned, continuous, naturally

40 Capitalization

1. Capitalize the first word of a sentence, the pronoun *I*, and the interjection *O*.

He enjoys science fiction, and so do **I**.
Psalm 3 says, "But thou, **O** Lord, art a shield for me."

2. Capitalize the first word of a direct quotation that is a complete sentence.

Wordsworth said of Wellington, "**P**oetically he may pass for a hero."

3. Capitalize the first word of every line of verse unless the poet has written the line with a lowercase letter.

Mary Coleridge's poem "The Deserted House" begins, "**T**here's no smoke in the chimney, / **A**nd the rain beats on the floor."

4. Capitalize proper nouns.

Millard **F**illmore

the **C**ivil **W**ar

5. Capitalize an official title when it precedes a name.

The graduation address was given by **S**enator Hernandez.

6. Capitalize the title of a high official when it is used in place of the person's name.

This morning the **P**resident signed the voting rights bill.

7. Capitalize abbreviations and designations that follow a name. Do not

capitalize titles used as appositives.

Maria Valdez, **Ph.D.**, a chemistry professor at the college, is on sabbatical this year.

8. Capitalize the title of a relative when it precedes a name or is used in place of a name. Do not capitalize the title if it is used with a possessive pronoun.

This photograph of the family includes **A**unt Paula but not my **u**ncle Phil.

9. Capitalize proper adjectives, except when they are part of compound nouns.

the **F**rench language   **f**rench fries
Venetian paintings   **v**enetian blinds

10. Capitalize the names of specific academic courses, but not general subject areas unless the area is a proper noun.

Physics 101   a **p**hysics lecture
Modern **E**nglish **P**oetry   an **E**nglish **p**oetry course

11. Capitalize names of the Deity, sacred books and other religious documents, religions, and religious denominations and their adherents.

the **L**ord   the **N**ew **T**estament
Judaism   **M**oslem

12. Capitalize the names of months, days, and holidays.

October   **F**riday   **T**hanksgiving

13. Capitalize the abbreviations A.D. and B.C.

A.D. 502   600 **B.C.**

14. For titles of literary works, capitalize the first and last words and all other important words, including prepositions of five or more letters. Capitalize both parts of a hyphenated word in a title.

Sir **G**awain and the **G**reen **K**night
The **B**erlitz **S**elf-**T**eacher
Gone with the **W**ind

(See Exercises 40-1 through 40-3.)

EXERCISE 40-1 | Capitals

Put capitals where necessary in the following sentences.

> **Example:** $\overset{M}{m}$rs. $\overset{S}{s}$mith is studying history and $\overset{G}{g}$erman.

1. the reading list for american literature 100 will include faulkner's *sanctuary* and ann tyler's *the accidental tourist.*

2. professors berry and oppenheim teach biology 301.

3. mr. hernandez graduated from the university of chicago.

4. julius caesar was killed in 44 b.c.

5. no one noticed that i had left the room.

6. would you like to eat breakfast now, grandfather?

7. last year aunt jane married my uncle bob.

8. william blake writes of the tiger, "what immortal hand or eye, / dare frame thy fearful symmetry?"

9. my danish friend has never heard of danish pastry.

10. the president of the united states will visit several countries, including belgium and italy.

EXERCISE 40-2 Capitals

Put capitals where necessary in the following sentences.

>   P   R
> *Example:*   professor rivera is meeting with three other professors.

1. all students at riverside university must take english, history, and math.

2. the finance committee is chaired by the congresswoman.

3. henry david thoreau urged, "cast your whole vote, not a strip of paper merely, but your whole influence."

4. the soccer championship was won by brazil.

5. the students in professor todaro's class are reading *the old man and the sea* by ernest hemingway.

6. kelly anderson, m.d., is a specialist in orthopedics.

7. shelters for the homeless are run by the lutheran, episcopal, and catholic churches.

8. the baptist choir practices every thursday evening.

9. mayor thorne will meet today with senator young.

10. in almost every south american country, spanish is spoken.

EXERCISE 40-3   Capitals

Put capitals where necessary in the following sentences.

>   H   D   C
> ***Example:*** her doctor wants her to see dr. castro for a second opinion.

1. sears tower in chicago is taller than the empire state building in new york.

2. charlemagne died in a.d. 814.

3. the book was written by alice reed, ph.d.

4. the old man scolded his son, "you have never done a day's work in your life, samuel."

5. the american revolution preceded the french.

6. the all-star game between the american league and the national league occurs halfway through the baseball season.

7. sonnet 130 by shakespeare ends "and yet, by heaven, i think my love as rare / as any she belied with false compare."

8. this committee will meet on the second tuesday of every month.

9. in this course, comparative religion, we will read parts of both the bible and the koran.

10. your power, o mighty god, is endless!

INDEX